A WEST CORK LIFE

Tina Pisco

RandomAnimals Press

Published 2003 by RandomAnimals Press

URL : www.awestcorklife.com

Copyright © Tina Pisco 2003

A catalogue record for this book is available from the British Library.

All Rights reserved

Cover design by John Noonan

Cover photos:
Graham Cooper (Francesca - Paddling Pool)
John Noonan (Grass And Nest)

Printed and bound in Great Britain by Cox & Wyman

About the Author

I moved with family from Brussels to Clonakilty in 1992.

Since then I have separated from my husband, been the Administrator of Craic na Coillte Street Theatre company, written freelance, worked in a hotel for cash, finished three novels and published two - not necessarily in that order.

I live in a big house on a hill in an isolated rural pocket of West Cork; with my daughters, our four dogs and three cats. I know it's an "isolated rural pocket" because every time a gale blows out the electrics, the ESB gets the power back on to everyone except those living in "isolated rural pockets".

After eleven years I'm about as settled as an urban nomad can ever be in a rural Irish village.

To John,

without whom this would not have been possible.

Table of Contents

Ackowlegement..1

A West Cork Life: 2002-2003...................7
   Spring Rallies and Plastic Bags..................9
   Of Daylight Saving Time, Housekeeping
   Rules, and the Law Of Residual Dirt........14
   Tis (almost) the Season of Spontaneous
   BBQs..19
   "Watch Out For That Cow!".......................24
   Free To A Good Home................................28
   "Roy Keane: ONE POINT. Roy Keane:
   UN POINT."..32
   Enough With The Rain Already!................37
   Summer? What Summer?..........................41
   Summer's End: It Ain't Over Till The Last
   Tourist Sings (at the Monday night trad'
   session)...42
   September Time-keeping and Science......46
   Arachnophobia Cured Here!......................50
   They Don't Make Stuff Like They Used
   To..55
   Tis The Pre-Season To Be Stressed Out.....59
   "If I Were You, I Wouldn't Start From
   Here."...64
   Winter Soltice..69
   I'm Dreaming Of A White Christmas........73

Table of Contents

Imbolc: Did St. Bridgit Detox?...................78
Forget Venus and Mars on Valentine's
Day...82
Nesting Instincts..86
The Woods Are Alive with the Sound of
Midgets..90
Pisco's Corollary and the Joys of Spring...95
Surviving the Plumbing Nightmare...........99
Happy Anniversary.....................................104

The Early Years:1993-1994ish.................109
   Chaos Management....................................111
   Happy B-Day To Me...................................117
   The Never-Ending Bedtime........................120
   Postpartum Awakening..............................125
   The Riddle of the Missing Sock.................129
   TipToe Through the Tomatoes...................133
   Wedding Bells and Holiday Hell...............138
   The Worst Thing About Having Kids........144

End Notes..151
   Goodbye to Father Eddie............................153
   Blown Away by West Cork.........................157
   A Taste of Duende.......................................161

Bare Bones Acknowledgement

If you're holding a book as you read this (as opposed to reading it off my computer screen) that means we actually made it- we produced a book. As I sit and write this introduction, achieving that goal isn't that obvious. In a typical West Cork way, what seemed like loads of time to finish a book last January has been pared down to a one week marathon race-to-the-finish deadline. In fairness now, it's hard to get things done in West Cork. Half the year you're so lethargic that you can barely get off the sofa to find the remote. The other half you're so busy that you cram 36 hours into each day. Then there's that little business of being happy. On the whole, people living in West Cork are happy to be here. Having a pretty good idea of what being happy feels like, and how to go about it, we tend to make time for it. Being happy a lot of the time means that it's one of the priorities in your scheduling. It's not for nothing that a West Cork motto is "Take yer time- but take it." Taking your time means sometimes deciding to go to the beach, or down to the pub, or over to visit some friends instead of working on your book (or garden, or whatever).

This book is special to me on many fronts. It's self-published. It's about West Cork. It's for West Cork.

Eleven years ago I moved here from Brussels. It may not seem like a very big move. Just a geographical hop for an urban nomad, who had spent her entire life moving from one city to another. But it was a fundamental life change. West Cork isn't just in a different time zone. It's in a different mind zone. I don't regret it. My only worry is that circumstance may some day force me to leave, and I'll have to live in a big city again. I dread the thought. I had always prided myself in being as adaptable as a tape worm- but now I know that I'm doomed to stay. In West Cork I finally found a place where I fit in. A place where I belong.

A West Cork Life

I finally understand why people have such trouble leaving their hometown. It's weird.

Being a writer I have written about my life in West Cork. Being a freelance writer I have sometimes managed to find people to pay me to write about it. Back in 1993, fresh off the ferry as it were, I had a column in the Cork Examiner under the name of Patsy Trench. I didn't use my real name so as not to embarrass my daughters. I stopped the column about a year later to write fiction. Last year, however, a small local newspaper called The West Cork Advertiser was launched. I was given the page-two column called "A West Cork Life". I write it under the name of Tina Pisco. I have, by now, embarrassed my daughters enough to not need a pen name.

The first section of the book, "A West Cork Life: 2002-2003" are those columns first published in the West Cork Advertiser. I'll take this opportunity to thank Linda O'Leary and all those involved with the West Cork Advertiser for reminding me how much I like writing columns. Above all I'd like to thank all of you who have read my column and given me so much positive encouragement. It's the comments every fortnight that make writing the column so much fun. I know this sounds a bit naff but I'm *really* glad you liked them. Readers in West Cork are the ones I want to please the most. By the by-thanks to Karin Jossels for suggesting I put a collection together.

So much happened in 2002-2003 that didn't get into the column: some great parties, terrific gigs, loads of fabulous music sessions (thanks to the lads at Scannell's for the Tuesday night blues session!), a production of "Annie", the National School's Easter Fair. Beaches and fishing. Paddy's Day and Halloween. The festival in the village. The war in Iraq. Births and deaths. Hellos and goodbyes.

The second section: "The Early Years 1993-94ish" are a few of my favourite Patsy Trench columns. The "End Notes" are bits I couldn't fit in the other two sections but wanted to include anyway.

This is where I get to thank people-which is both delightful and a bummer. It's delightful because only writers really get the chance to thank people in print. It's a bummer because you always forget someone. The list is too long to ever be complete. It would have to include most of the people I meet in the course of my day. It's part of the beauty of living here: friends and neighbours you could thank everyday. So, here in no particular order are just a few of the people who deserve a mention (If your name isn't here, please excuse me. Space was tight.):

A West Cork Life

Clo, Amel, Sash, Fresca, Ray and John, who were often the first to read these before I sent them off to the Advertiser. You are my life and you know it. Elaine Walsh and all my other friends and neighbours in the village. All my friends, buddies, and mates in Clon'. RandomAnimals: Mark and Niamh; Martin and Sheila; James and Denise. The Bank of Ireland, Clonakilty, for their continuing faith and support. Paul Campbell (and Steph!) for coming to the rescue several times this year. Thanks also to John Spillane whose lyrics are sprinkled in several columns. You say it so well. Finally, John Noonan deserves an extra mention for all the work he did to put this book together. His contribution is impossible to measure but includes formatting the book, finding a printer, getting the specs right, typesetting it, designing the cover, and loving me.

June 2003

A WEST CORK LIFE

2002-2003

These first appeared in the West Cork Advertiser.

Spring Rallies and Plastic Bags

Spring comes early to West Cork. The rains still lash down, the winds can still chill you to the bone, and some years a sudden snowfall can cover the hills in a soft white blanket, but the land knows it's all a sham. The worst is past. To the eye that doesn't see, the hills look just as barren as they did in December and the summer seems far away. But every day the sun rises a little earlier and sets a little later. And the buds and the birds, and every living thing, soak up each small extra dose of sunlight like nectar.

In other parts of Europe, Spring officially starts on March 21st, but over here we're in full swing by then. St. Bridgit's Day back at the beginning of February marks the beginning of the season. The first January I lived here I was bemoaning the cold days ahead to a lovely old lady from Ardfield. "Cheer up" she said. "It'll soon be over. Another ten days and it'll be Spring" I thought she was a bit batty at the time, until I saw the daffodils blooming in February.

This year the Winter was so mild that the camellias got their schedules mixed up and were spilling flowers down the road well before the daffs were in bloom. The bottom of the drive looked as if two ballroom dancing contestants had come to blows, leaving a carpet of shredded pink petals behind. The daffs are in full bloom now, the primroses are peeking out of the hedgerows, and crows crisscross the skies transporting what look like two-by-fours.

In West Cork there is another sure sign that Spring has arrived. You wake up one morning and hear something strange. Drowning out the birdsong is the sound of revving motors - and that's just the guys who've come to watch, not the contestants. The West Cork Rally has arrived and with it the knowledge that the tourist season is upon us again. It will grow in small increments of English and Welsh until it peaks somewhere at the end of July, when you'll have to elbow your way through hordes of Spanish and Italians wearing designer tweed caps (God bless'em), and you won't be able to swing a cat on the main street without hitting a geranium.

One thing that won't be blooming as much this year is the traditional crop of plastic bags festooning the hedgerows and trees. After much hesitation, the government finally decided to introduce the plastic bag levy. The fifteen-cent tax was meant to encourage people to use less plastic bags as well as raise money for the environment. They probably paid coach loads of experts masses of money to study the impact of this type of legislation. I wonder if any of them predicted what would happen. I have no idea how things went up in the Big Smoke, but down here it was quite astounding. People simply stopped using plastic bags. Altogether. Overnight. From one day to the next.

Like many of my friends and neighbours, I rooted out my old straw basket, bought a big reusable bag, stuffed it with old plastic ones, and promptly forgot them in the car when I went out shopping. For about a week I kept bumping into people juggling their loaves of bread and bottles of milk as I tried to balance my shopping with a frozen pizza tucked under one arm and the paper stuffed up my armpit. But we soldiered on. By and by we got used to the new regime. People proudly produced a manky plastic bag and were congratulated for it. Shopkeepers started keeping a pile of handy small boxes for the likes of me, who were still forgetting our brand new reusable shopping bags. In the car park of a major chain in Bishopstown, trolleys were laden with a collection of mismatched boxes, bags, and cartons. Chic Brown Thomas tote-bags snuggled up to garish Aldi bags. Pennys and Dunnes thought nothing of sharing a trolley with Tescos.

A local shopkeeper told me that she had not sold more than seven plastic bags in a week. "I usually sell that many in an hour. People just refuse to buy them." We both agreed that it was a good thing and that those who thought that people were too cheap to buy them had got it wrong. People really do care about the environment- sometimes all you have to do is make it a little easier for them to do the right thing. All it took was one little push and "Hey Presto!"-people changed their behavior.

"Imagine the amount of plastic bags that won't end up in the rubbish from this shop alone," I commented as I picked up my purchases and piled them carefully one on top of the other.

"Absolutely," she said, opening the door for me. "They should have done it years ago. Are you sure you can manage?"

"I'm grand," I answered, feeling very noble as I kept a yoghurt balanced with my chin. "If I can just remember to take the bags out of the car I'll be flying it."

March 2002

Of Daylight Saving Time, Housekeeping Rules, and the Law of Residual Dirt.

Last Sunday the powers that be did it again: They changed the clocks. Not that it makes much of a difference to my time-keeping. Like most of my friends I don't wear a watch. West Cork must be one of the few places in Western Europe where fifteen people sitting around a table can be hard pressed to tell you the exact time. Thankfully most pubs have a clock right behind the bar for those of us who have something to do that requires knowing the precise time: like catching a bus, say.

So the clocks went back (I think). I get caught out every year- twice if you count when they put them forward again (if I got it wrong don't bother to write. Like not wearing a watch, I can't be bothered to remember little rhymes about whether we are falling forward or springing backwards - Thanks).

I believe all this clock shuffling is supposed to have something to do with energy saving, or milking cows or some other EU regulation. Whatever. In my life it all has to do with housekeeping.

I hate it in the Autumn. On an unsuspecting Sunday the back of the house suddenly disappears into the shadows for the winter. It's depressing. By three o'clock in what used to be the afternoon, we are plunged into darkness. This means you're doing laundry in the middle of the night. The up side is that you can't possibly do anything like sweeping or cleaning out the cobwebs as you can't see them.

Then five months later- BAM!

I used to think that Spring-cleaning had something to do with rebirth and renewal. That was before I lived in a big stone house in the middle of the countryside. Spring is the first time in months that there is enough light to see the dirt. Spring fever might mean prancing hares and nesting birds outside, but inside it means an irrepressible desire to actually look under things.

Suddenly I'm at it. Hauling piles of newspapers nobody noticed accumulating in the back hall, clearing out cupboards, and washing out corners. The much-misused phrase: "You don't want to go there!" was actually invented to describe the corners of my house after the Winter. In a house like mine you could devote a whole day just to cobwebs. The new light illuminates them and you recoil in horror at the grey tents above your head. Dust "bunnies", which sound cute and harmless, have evolved like evil Pokemons into Dust Dinosaurs that are actually quite frightening.

The task at hand is so overwhelming that I have evolved some general rules and theories to help me cope. Anything that aides procrastination is a benefit, for once you start Spring Cleaning you are on the treadmill to Housekeeping Hell.

The First Rule of Housekeeping is this: Pay someone else to do it. I'm not kidding. This is a job worthy of the Army Civil Engineering Corps (with a little help from the Bomb Disposal Unit for the really icky things lurking in the garage) and should be justly rewarded. In our economy we justly reward people by paying them. If you can afford it that's the only rule you need to know.

Rule Two: Take a deep cleansing breath. Accept that if you live in an old stone house you will NEVER get it clean. Never. It makes dirt for a living.

Rule Three: put on some really loud music. This will lift your spirits and drown out your grumbling.

Rule Four:
   4.1. Hoover it up.
   4.2. If you can't hoover it up: Paint over it.

Housekeeping is heartbreaking at best. You're battling the Second Law of Thermodynamics with a pan and brush. You're going to lose! (I'm not going to explain. I only have 800 words in this column. Look it up.) Also I find that I like tasks that require minimum effort for maximum effect. Housekeeping does not qualify. In fact its dangerous to apply this to cleaning a house. You think you'll just tidy up a bit and not give it a good clean until the end of the week (or the end of the Winter). But then you hit the Law of Residual Dirt:

    New dirt accumulates at a regular rate. Everyday the house gets a little dirtier. You'd think that if you tidy up a bit each day you'd keep the flow at bay. But no. That's because Residual Dirt (the dirt that's left behind) grows twice as fast as good clean new dirt. Moreover Residual Dirt has amazing properties. After a few days it mimics the primeval ooze and creates new life. Molds and slimes come first, followed by mosses and primitive forests. Left to its own devices it will develop its own civilization within a month and you will have to call in the sanitation department to deal with the new life-forms camping in the downstairs toilet.

April 2002

Tis (almost) the Season of Spontaneous BBQs

The weather was so wonderful last week that it was easy to sit in a sunny corner, sheltered from the wind, and forget that the night before temperatures had dropped to below freezing. Some days it varied from 16C to -1C in twelve hours. So bring out the shorts and pile on the duvets- its April.

In West Cork one afternoon of serious sunshine is all it takes. People stroll around in skimpy clothes with the first rays. Like the landscape, they take very little notice of how hot or cold it actually is. Give'em some extra hours of sun and they behave as if we all live in the Canaries. One of the sure ways to spot a tourist is to look for the guy in the Aran jumper.

Young people are particularly immune to the cold in any season. Hardy teenagers hang around on street corners with little more than a T-shirt to protect them from the wind. At least some of the lads have the sense to throw on a light jacket. Their female contemporaries shiver in teeny-tiny tops, their exposed midriffs blue and goose-bumped.

Actually I read somewhere that your reaction to cold is linked to where you spend the first few years of your life. It has something to do with the growth of fat cells, or sweat glands, or some other bodily function. That is why an African, for example (or me for that matter), will always be cold in Ireland, even in the summer; while the locals run around red-faced and "roastin" whenever a heat wave of 24C hits our shores. Believe me- you don't know what a heat wave is until the thermometer starts creeping towards 40C.

Still the portents are good for the summer. Frog spawn was spotted in the fuladh fía at Drombeg stone circle as early as March. Dolphins have been coming into various bays, and a tadpole was sighted last week. All, I am told, omens of balmy days on the beach to come. Not that I'd know- I just fervently wish they are right. A good summer in West Cork is hard to beat. But whatever the weather we'll do our best to prove that we're the "Riviera" of this island.

One of the great things about a West Cork summer is the Spontaneous BBQ. As its name suggests this is not a planned event. The earliest one can receive notice is late that morning. Early evening, just before ordering the last round in the beer garden, is traditional. This allows drinking-up time to decide who will nip over to the shop, who will be hosting, and to count up how many children will be attending (Ten is average. Children in West Cork come in packs.). Seeing as the sun was shining, last Saturday was the perfect time to herald in the 2002 season.

We got the call in the morning and arrived a few hours later bearing a packet of sausages and beer. The more resourceful brought salad and wine. Sitting out on a rooftop deck, nestled above the town, it was a delightful afternoon. As one friend happily declared: "It must be summer- we're sitting outside in the sun, freezing our bums, and eating burnt food!" Just a taste of the months to come, one hopes.

When we weren't lolling around in the sun last week, those of us who have a garden were getting in touch with Nature. Though in my case getting to grips is more appropriate. To be perfectly honest the word "garden" does not really apply. Overgrown jungle would probably be more accurate, though I personally like to think of it as an EU Very Small Area of Scientific Interest. Managing a chunk of West Cork wilderness is like wrestling a tree. Literally. I do not pretend to force my will on the land. After all I am only one woman with a slasher against the Forces of Nature. There are plants growing in the woods that look like extras in the Day of the Triffids.

I try instead to engage in a benevolent containment policy. This has to be timed very carefully as you only really get between now and the end of May to have any long-term effect. By mid-June the growth rate is astronomical. If I don't go mano a mano with it now, the brambles will sneak up to the house one night in July and engulf it. We will have to use a machete to get down the drive.

Then again the place is a haven for birds, butterflies, badgers, and foxes. As I have very little input in the "garden", walking around outside is always a surprise. You never know where a bank of foxgloves might pop up this year. It always feels like a gift to find that a blackthorn has decided to grow on a wall, or that wild roses have beat the brambles in a sunny corner, or that primroses have taken advantage of the clearing created by cutting down a tree last Autumn. Best of all I never have to mow the lawn.

April 2002

"Watch Out For That Cow!"

They're back! I don't care that I've been freezing my bum for the past week, or that hailstones slowed traffic to a halt today, seeing them swoop and dive always makes my heart light. "L'Hirondelle ne fait pas le printemps" is a French saying about how just because you see a swallow doesn't mean it's Spring. Rubbish. As far as I'm concerned that's a typical case of French pragmatic pessimism. It's also wrong. I don't know what they mean in Provence, but for me swallows are by far the most accurate season-predictor West Cork's got to offer. After all you sure can't go by the weather.

The first time I see swallows performing

A West Cork Life

aerial manouvers over the front field I know that Spring is here, even if it's as miserable as a wet Tuesday in November. When I see them start lining up on the telephone wire outside my bedroom window, I know that Autumn's just around the corner. In between you get Summer- if you're lucky.

We went on holiday in Tunisia at the end of April a few years back. We were delighted to see the swallows congregating everywhere as they got ready to move North for the Summer. We found it amusing to think that maybe the very same birds hanging out by the pool watching Ireland get creamed by Germany in wasser-polo, would be practicing their flying skills over our house in a few weeks time. We marveled at the fact that they would fly all that way to find last year's nests in the garage and sheds, and giggled at the thought that the swallows were going on their annual bird package holiday to Ireland. So when a few weeks after our return we saw the first swallows swoosh overhead we got to thinking that this was the advance party getting everything ready. Since then I always see the first swallows as little Bird-Tours reps with tiny shamrock emblazoned T-shirts, humming "The Fields of Athenry".

In a few weeks the sky will be full of them. And I know few things finer than lying in the front field on a sunny day and watching them as they spin high in the blue or dive bomb to inches off the ground and skim over the grass. But as I wax lyrical about the simple joys of life in the countryside I know that not everyone appreciates them. I was reminded of that fact recently with a perfect example of the Nervous Visitor. You've seen the type - maybe even some of your family and friends qualify. They live stressful lives in stressful cities and have such a stressful time of it that they are totally stressed out. Things that I take for granted as part and parcel of country living can totally freak a Nervous Visitor. They come over to relax and they spend a lot of time worrying -mainly about dangers that in the city might be relevant but, over here, are wildly out of context. I find myself trotting out a litany of reassurances: "Old houses make odd noises at night. It's the plumbing. Dogs bark for all sorts of reasons. Yes I suppose there probably is something out there in the dark woods. It's probably a fox. No foxes aren't dangerous. Ireland doesn't have rabies. Or predators. Or snakes." Do you tell them the truth the whole truth and nothing but the truth about the mice situation? Three cats are pretty good at keeping out mice but you never know when one might decide to stroll in and have a look around.

A West Cork Life

Nervous Visitors worry about driving on the left-hand side of the road. They worry about walking on country lanes. They worry about security even though their own neighborhood crime rate probably exceeds that of County Cork. They ask safety questions all day long. Lying in the field on a sunny day, the Nervous Visitor would probably worry about whether a swallow could take out your eye ("No, I honestly don't think so."), or whether there are any horrible creepy-crawlies that could bite ("Creepie-crawlies? Baby, there are stinging plants in the grass that could put an insect to shame.")

When I get fed up being the Local Rural Reassurance Officer (or LORRO-which, funnily enough, means parrot in Spanish), I tell them that they are being silly-there are far more dangerous things to worry about in the countryside. Like flying cows. I personally know two women who were hit by a cow as they were driving along. Presumably the cow jumped over a low wall and landed on their car. Luckily they both recovered. That usually stops the Nervous Visitor from asking safety questions while I drive as they are too busy watching out for low-flying cows. Keeps them quiet and me happy.

May 2002

Free To A Good Home

We have four new arrivals in the house this week. Our "kitten" had kittens. Affectionately known as "Roadkill" (we found her while driving home one night), she hasn't grown much and is still only about half the size of the other two cats. Somehow we failed to note that she was getting up to more mischief than just chasing birds and opening the fridge. It was definitely a teen pregnancy. We didn't even notice that she was getting tubby until a week ago but she seems to have managed quite well. Knock me down with a feather and call me a softie, but there're few domestic animals as cute as newborn kittens. I think its because kittens are so incredibly tiny yet quite obviously cats. These four guys are about the size of a lighter. They're mini-cats.

As far as I'm concerned puppies only come a close second in the pet-cuteness stakes (In the wild, fox cubs rule). We've been blessed by quite a number of six-pack bundles of fur in our time, so the novelty has probably worn off. Thanks to the intervention of modern science our puppy days are over, but we have in the past been littered with them. Puppies are feisty and fast long before they can learn anything useful like "Stay". When you've got half a dozen careening around they can add a great deal of confusion to a house that is bordering on the edge of chaos at the best of times. Six puppies tearing through the place can make a three-year old's birthday party look like a meeting of the Catatonic Society. They also love following you around. Actually they don't follow so much as slalom between your feet nipping at your ankles and each other. It makes getting the shopping out of the car like dancing a jig on a tightrope while balancing heavy bags.

One summer we had seven puppies. They folllowed us everywhere. The only way to go for a walk alone was to feed the puppies out the back, then walk quickly yet nonchalantly into the house (not run or they'd think you wanted to race), climb out the kitchen window, and leg it down the front field before they finished eating and noticed you'd gone. Getting into the car and driving away was a two-man operation. The Driver would slowly back the car, as the Puppy-Meister raced the puppies to the backfield. The Driver would then maneuver the car into position on the drive and beep the horn. This was the Puppy-Meister's cue to fill a bowl with puppy food and leg it. Jumping into the car as the Driver burned rubber required superior teamwork, combining a good level of fitness with precision driving skills. Timing was of the essence. A ten second delay and at best you could start the whole process again. At worst, you'd have to try and catch six puppies running off down the road. If, in the anxiety of the moment, someone forgot to close the house door properly the consequences hit somewhere around 7.6 on the Richter scale. I recall one incident where the puppies managed to redecorate the house with shredded toilet paper, the contents of the rubbish, and a surprising number of cuddly toys. Still I must admit that it gave me great pleasure to go to school the next morning and ask the teacher to excuse my daughter because the dogs ate her homework. It felt like I'd looked up and seen a pig fly. I will say this much for puppies: If you could invent a toy that is as much fun as half a dozen puppies you'd put Fisher-Price out of business. Puppies are the ultimate interactive toys.

Mind you kittens aren't half bad in the entertainment department. A kitten and a ball of string are a classic comedy duo. Best of all house training a kitten consists in showing it the cat-box or the door as the case may be. ("Over there? You want me to do it over there? OK.") That's basically all it takes.

The kittens were born while I was in town. I returned to find that the household pet population had almost doubled. The cats have finally achieved parity (and then some) with the dogs. Of course that means the pets now grossly outnumber the humans. We're only head to head at the best of times- a pony in the backfield and the pets win. It's a good thing that about a dozen family members intend to visit this summer or the animals might start getting notions. Then again our newbies should be gone by the end of July. I'm hoping that it'll be easy to find homes for them (seeing as they're so incredibly cute and all). Four mini-cats. Two ginger. Two tortoise-shell. Ready to go in about eight weeks.

May 2002

"Roy Keane: ONE POINT. Roy Keane: UN POINT."

Every four years a terrible sense of alienation descends upon me. It's as if I'm living in a parallel world surrounded by green bunting. The World Cup is on again. I walk into pubs and am greeted by yells to "Sit down!" I can't join in the conversations. I miss out on the camaraderie of my friends. But this year is different. Thanks to Roy Keane, I can finally participate in the World Cup. At last I have something I can talk about with the rest of the Nation. Which is good because this week Roy Keane was the only thing the Nation wanted to talk about. I travelled from Cork to Dublin and back and, except for a few cursory remarks about the terrible weather, no one talked about anything else. Every Dublin taxi man had his own version of "what really happened". These ranged from the imminent birth of Roy's illegitimate child, to Roy's fear of flying. I joined in the discussions with gusto. Finally, here was a subject related to football that I could grasp. I didn't feel left out.

The fact is that I know nothing about sport. I am aware that for most of you this is totally anathema but it's the guilty truth. It's not that I don't like sports. It's a cultural thing. My family never watched sport. We didn't have a family team we supported. We never knew the joy of jumping around the telly screaming "Ole! Ole! Ole!" because our team won. It's not that we didn't jump around screaming "Ole! Ole!" mind you. I remember one occasion when we yelled the house down. But it wasn't for sport. It was for the Eurovision Song Contest when Spain won with "La La La La".

The Eurovision Song Contest is a family tradition. Since the first one I can remember (Black and white telly. Switzerland won.) it has brought us together on the couch like no other program can. It's a tradition that I've kept up with my own brood. So its no surprise that last Saturday night (while the rest of the Nation discussed Roy Keane) we all got comfy to enjoy this year's Eurovision Song Contest.

I have to say that it was a peach. Now don't get me wrong- a large part of the contest's appeal is its total naffness. This year's event in Estonia had us helpless with laughter. From the circa 1975 Eastern European Barbie and Ken presenters, to the Disco Tour of Baltic Pop it was a total hoot. By the time the Slovenian drag queens took to the stage we were gasping for breath. I believe they were singing about an airline. There was a definite airplane theme. They were dressed in sparkly red airhostess costumes and had dance moves that appeared to be indicating the Exits. It was classic Eurovision- right up there with the Finnish entry one year which had a catchy tune sung by a Laplander in traditional costume, accompanied by his reindeer.

This year many countries decided to sing in English- which only added to the entertainment. I don't want to appear snooty-after all every democratic country has a right to cheesy pop, but the grammatical convolutions of some of the lyrics were only topped by the dance routines. So much for Europe's pride in its regional languages. I was pleased, however, to see that some Eurovision traditions remain. The French judge refused to speak English and the mantra of, "Germany three points.

L'Allemagne trois points," was as soothing as a childhood lullaby.

Once the voting started it was clear that it was going to be a two-horse race. Malta and Latvia were going to battle it out. No one else stood a chance- not even the Russian boy band (God love'em. I think they inherited Boyzone's white outfits from an early tour). As the voting progressed we started to favor Latvia. When The Former Yugoslavian Republic of Macedonia put Latvia one point ahead we knew we'd backed a winner, though we had to wait through excruciating tension until the very last vote (Latvia: TWELVE POINTS! La Latvie: DOUZE POINTS!) to see "I Wanna" crowned Eurovision song 2002.

By the by -I know our friends in Eastern Europe have had a rotten time of it and have been fairly busy, but you'd think they'd get around to renaming a country properly. The Former Yugoslavian Republic of Macedonia (FYR Macedonia for short) is rather a mouthful. It also has an unfortunate resemblance to The Artist Formerly Known as Prince. It's as if they couldn't think of a new name but didn't want the old one either. Most new countries find a different name (Zaire) or stick republic in front of the old one (Ireland). Imagine being called The Country That Used To Be Called

Ireland (TCTUTBC Ireland). "Hail the country that used to be called Ireland!..." just doesn't cut it as a rousing chorus no matter who's Captain of the football team.

May 2002

Enough With The Rain Already!

Ok I've had it. I wish to register a complaint: What the hell happened to the weather? The summer solstice is this Friday but its going to take a flame-thrower and a few minor explosives if we're going to have any chance of lighting a bonfire. Where are the hot sunny days I was looking forward to when this paper started up? Where are the spontaneous BBQs? Why aren't I on a boat fishing and getting a tan? It's the end of June, and I've sat in a beer garden just the once! What happened to lazy afternoons on the beach followed by lazy evenings sitting outside? Why am I still wearing a jumper? I mean, I know the Emerald

Isle has a unique melancholy beauty in the rain, but enough already! Is there a government department in charge? Could it possibly be under the Department of Arts Culture and the Gaeltacht? Tourism? After all they're both in the melancholy misty Green Theme Park business. Doesn't the weather come under Bord Failte's brief (Cead Mile Failte- here's a complimentary umbrella). Surely they have a responsibility to our foreign visitors who read the brochures, booked two weeks in Ireland and are presently standing at Moll's Gap taking pictures of the scenic fog at their feet. I feel for those poor guys on the bicycle tours staring at their laminated maps, as buckets of water pour off their plastic ponchos. I want to know who's in charge because if there's some Junior Minister out there that I can belt, I want to make sure to get him before he boards his flight to the Canaries.

Memories of last summer haunt me. I shake my head and wonder if it was all a dream. Did we really sit outside until three o'clock in the morning and not get hypothermia? Was that me swimming in the sea? In a bathing suit? With a tan? Surely not. Aye there's the rub. T'was not a dream but a reality that comforted us through a mild winter with the promise that another great summer was on the way. But that's not how it works in West Cork. Someone once told me that you only get a great summer every five years. The other four years you get a few so-so summers (to keep you from falling into a permanent depression) and a few summers that really suck. The problem is that we suffer from collective selective amnesia. That one great summer is so spectacular that it carries you through the bad summers in the hope that you'll get just one measly week, one weekend, maybe an afternoon of former glory. Because let's face it - when we do get the weather Crete has nothing on West Cork. Summer '95 was so good I waited patiently for it to happen again for six years. At the moment it's a toss up for summer 2002. There's still a smidgen of hope for July but its getting fainter each time I navigate through the floodwater that used to be the road up to my house. I think I've finally accepted that unless we have a U-turn in the sunshine (Please, please, please) at best we'll have a so-so summer. I just pray that we get all the fine days in a row; not dotted over the next two months. One solid week of beach can make up for a string of miserable Sundays. The worst thing about the odd fine day is that they always fall on a day when I have loads to do indoors. Mind you, after ten summers I should know that the West Cork Summer Rule is: Drop everything you're doing and head to the beach the minute it gets warm enough to do so.

We got conned this year. We were ready for summer. Winter was a peach. Spring jumped in real early. It was going so well. The flowers were blooming, the birds were singing, the temperature was rising nicely and then one afternoon sometime last month it started to rain. What happened? I distinctly remember driving back from Drimoleague on a beautiful Thursday morning in early May with the sun-roof open and smelling summer on its way. Where'd it go? Did it just veer off course and head South? Did it decide to give us a miss altogether?

I think we should all get some sort of State Compensation. It's bad enough being out of the World Cup without being cold and wet to boot. I mean let's face it -we've been stoic. We've smiled at the tourists and family visitors and made encouraging sounds through the wettest month of May since 1931 and we're plum out of happy noises.

June 2002

Summer? What Summer?

We have visitors. Lots of them. It's cold. It's still raining.

Enough said.

July 2002

Summer's End: It Ain't Over Till The Last Tourist Sings (At The Monday Night Trad' Session)

With the sun finally out, and throngs of tourists still walking around taking pictures of flower boxes, its hard to admit that summer's end is at hand. But, let's face it guys it's the last hurrah. I'm just grateful that we got a few days we could actually call summer after the buckets of rain that fell in May, June, and most of July.

The signs are all there. Little signs that you could easily miss but which you cannot deny if you live in the countryside. After ten years here the landscape has carved a space in my senses whose sole function is to perceive the changing seasons. It is as physical as hearing, or tasting, or seeing, and I can no more avoid sensing the coming of Winter, or Spring, than I can avoid feeling a chill in the air or seeing a flash of lightning.

You smell it first. Women in town comment on it. "The summer's over. I could smell it this morning," we repeat, nodding to each other in resignation. We know in our bones that school runs and dark evenings are on the way.

Other signs start to make an appearance. The field in front of my house develops a ghostly mist each time the breeze rustles through it as every manner of dandelion, thistles or other fluffy white thing blows away from its stalk. Caterpillars lounge fat and furry in the heat of the sun. The wild roses on the beach have lost their paper-thin pink petals, sporting ugly swollen purple rose hips instead that look like they belong on a witch's nose. This is also the time of the year for the best, the brightest, the most golden sunsets. And they're coming in at around eight in the evening which is a far more reasonable time for a sunset than eleven o'clock at night. They herald the more sensible time ahead when we stop all this silly summer partying and get on with the business of making a living and getting kids educated.

Inland, where the sea breeze reaches only when the wind blows from the South, you can smell Autumn sooner than on the coast. Spring comes very early to West Cork but so does Autumn. Other countries lull you into believing that summer will last forever with flashy bursts in August. Not here, baby. By August 20th it is undeniable. Autumn is standing in the wings yelling: "Go on! Go Home! Get back on the bus we're closing down for the winter!"

Mind you this summer was hardly a season at all. We stoically had spontaneous BBQ's under dark and menacing skies and went hoarse yelling at children to put on a jumper. Last week's day spent roasting in a beautiful cove, as the ocean lapped lightly on the rocks, was just a cruel reminder of what we missed this year.

When I first feel the summer starting to ebb, I can sense the winter coming up the road, just round the bend, and I shudder. I think to myself that I can't stand another winter in West Cork. But then, little by little, I start to look forward to it: The smell of early mornings in November, the way the fields look with a touch of frost on a sunny winter's day, the crackle of the fire, and the comfort meeting friends in the pub on a cold and wet afternoon. I figure the year that doesn't happen is the Autumn I move to Arizona, or Morocco, or some other place on the planet where it's summer all the year round. But for now I get a perverse pleasure out of imagining myself in December, in the yard, battling the elements in a raging gale. Well, maybe just the once.

August 2002

September Time-keeping and Science

Right so: We finally got that whole going back to school business finished and thank God for that. The books and uniforms are sorted, the inevitable difficulties of imposing a schedule on a household that has been sleeping in for the last two months have been conquered, and life has finally settled back into a somewhat orderly progression. In town you don't have to fight your way through delegations of tourists as they wander about, there are more than enough stools up at the bar, and you don't have to drive three times around the one way system to find a parking place. The last of the visitors have been packed up and sent back to their home countries and wouldn't you know it- that's when the weather finally decided to give us a treat. Still the peace and quiet that now descends on my house at around 9:30 on weekday mornings was worth the wait. Much as I love the summer I have to admit that this is probably my favorite time of year: when the light is like Golden syrup on the landscape and the proportion of day to night is as it should be. Of course in two months time there won't be much that you can actually call "day". Blink and it'll be over.

At this time of the year, however, you have clearly defined mornings, afternoons, evenings, and nights. Being a rather disorganised person by nature who (to make matters worse) works from home, I fully appreciate the clear-cut timekeeping of the Autumn. It makes it so much easier to differentiate when I should be doing what. Household duties are best performed in the morning, working carries me through to mid-afternoon when children occupy most of my time, evenings are for eating dinner and leisure, and nighttime is for sleeping. In the summer there is no such thing as the "evening". You go along your day and before you know it its twelve o'clock at night. It's as if you loose an entire time slot. Sometime in September you see reappear that blessed time between

5pm and 10pm which can be put to good use pottering around, making dinner, or watching the television as the fire crackles happily in the hearth.

I don't watch much television in the summer (see above) and I must admit that returning to the box after a few months absence I am alarmed to see a significant increase in the use of fake science in advertisements. It was bad enough being subjected to the threat of children succumbing to the dreadful Fading Disease if we didn't buy a certain dairy product, now they want to dazzle us with numbers. For those of you who don't know what I'm talking about: the Fading Disease is a condition that makes children fade into a pale grey shadow of their former selves due to the nasty purple bouncing balls invading their poor little under immunised systems. Thankfully this can be countered by buying the said dairy product which fills up the child with a wall of cheerful yellow balls that keep the purple balls at bay. Clearly the powers that be in ad agencies have decided that fancy pants computer graphics aren't enough to convince us of the serious "scientific" reasons for buying their products. No, now they can calculate it for us. So far I have noted that there are seven signs of aging, six signs of healthy hair, and 99 stains that taint my laundry. 99? How can they be so sure? Whatever happened to "As easy as 1,2,3!" or even "Presto! It's clean!" I find myself wondering what those 99 stains are. I want to see the list. I assume that it includes old classics like grass stains, ketchup and blood but what about biro? What about mango juice? What about slurry? Have they finally found a way to get rid of permanent black marker? I'm waiting for a rival washing powder to up the ante: CLEANS 101 STAINS.

As if mothers didn't have enough to be worrying about; what with preventing their children from fading away while combating the seven signs of aging and maintaining the six signs of healthy hair. Now we must worry if that weird purple smear on little Johnny's shirt is covered by the 99 Official Stains Act.

As for using famous footballer's wives to advertise this new advance in laundry technology, frankly I'm not impressed. She is admittedly lovely and looks well pleased to tell us that the 99 stains have finally been vanquished but I ask you: why is she doing the laundry, and would her family ever just pick up after themselves? Surely a man who plays for Ireland can afford some home help and learn not to leave his dirty clothes on the floor?

September 2002

Arachnophobia Cured Here!

The fog rolled in and landed on my doorstep yesterday morning. The outside world disappeared into a fuzzy grey haze and the house felt as if it was floating in the clouds. The wind and rain followed today. I expect the temperature to finally drop dramatically over the weekend. Not that I'm getting into the forecasting business or anything. It's just that the weather has been so glorious this month that it was easy to ignore the leaves littering the drive. The light was exceptional this September as Autumn entered the scene in a blaze of glory. Hanging on to the last rays of sunshine I ignored the signs that clearly indicated it was time to get out the jumpers, find the wellies, and collect the coats from the dry cleaning where they've hung forgotten over the summer. It's been happening for over a month, but its really only this week that I've noticed that the landscape has changed to muted browns and russets, ochre and sienna. The forty shades of green have moved left on the color chart: more olive and loden than apple or Kelly. Of course warm days and spectacular sunsets haven't fooled the wild animals. They know that winter is on its way and they're busy getting ready for the long sleep. They're out and about, stocking up on food and finding winter accommodation. This is one of the best times of the year for Wildlife Watch- a game played as we drive around the country roads in the dark. Hedgehogs give each other the word and go walkabout. It's like they're visiting all their friends and relations before curling up and going to sleep for the winter. Some nights we've spotted three or four ambling down the roads. Foxes and badgers are also out and about more than at other times, and we even saw a small stoat dragging a bunny across the road the other day.

Many small creatures that crawl, creep, slither or slide are looking for a warm, dry place to spend the winter months. I suppose it's not surprising that some of them look up, see our house poking out of the fog and think: "Hey! That looks cosy. Betcha those people are the types who forget to put the cheese back in the fridge! I wonder if they're following the Sopranos?" And so they come.

The butterflies flutter through the house as they desperately try and find a place to fold up their wings and not move for a few months. In past years they've been particularly attracted to the laundry room. We have had up to seven butterflies tucked into a corner of the shelves. I don't know if it's the heat, the humidity, or the reassuring Aloe Vera Aqua Non-Bio Spring Fresh smell that attracts them. We would also be a big neon "VACANCY" sign for rats if it weren't for the dogs. Should one venture near the house it will be immediately caught, killed, and lovingly deposited on my doorstep as a present. Mice also find the house attractive. So do slugs and spiders. The mice are cute little escapees from a Beatrix Potter book. I deal with them pragmatically by having three cats. Three is the magic number when it comes to cats and mice in this house. I have only ever seen a slug once when I came down at three in the morning for a glass of water, but the slimy trails on the kitchen walls are evidence that they probably have raves in there at night.

A West Cork Life

I have as yet not really bothered to find a way to get rid of them. I suspect it would mean choosing between injecting chemicals into the walls or leaving bowls of beer out at night. Unlike the slugs, the spiders are spectacular and not at all shy. We call the really big ones Wolf Spiders. I don't know if this is a scientifically accurate name but it sounds right. We treat them with the respect they deserve. We catch them in a glass and put them outside. I'm actually quite fond of them unless they're hanging on the ceiling above my head. I figure they, like the cats and dogs, keep the ecology of the house from evolving into a rodent and bug paradise.

While I'm on the subject of mice I feel I should point out that there is nothing to be afraid of. I apologise to all those who run screaming from these tiny furry mammals- but it doesn't make any sense at all. In the unlikely scenario that a mouse might bite you, you probably wouldn't notice. I say unlikely because you'd have to trap a mouse in your hand to get him to bite you which is unlikely if you're the type of person who runs straight through a plate glass window at the first suspicion of a squeak. If, however, you were to accidentally step on one, you'd probably flatten it. Please note the politically correct gender parity in my mouse comments. The fact that I have never known a man to run screaming down the drive because he saw a mouse, makes no difference. I'm sure there's one out there somewhere (All letters welcome. Anonymity assured). One man I know- who shan't be named- was so scared of spiders that he had been known to overturn furniture in his frantic attempt to flee the room during a showing of Arachnophobia. He is, may I add, now perfectly cured. A few years back at this time of year, the girls decided to give him a huge wolf spider in a box. The spider jumped out and raced straight for his throat. I don't know if it was coming face to face with his worst nightmare and surviving, or the humiliation of having very small girls rolling around laughing at him that did it- but he now calmly catches spiders with the rest of us and puts them outside.

October 2002

They Don't Make Stuff Like They Used To

The weather finally got nippy this week. Though the sun is still giving us some beautiful days, the desire to stay home is growing as the winter hibernation period descends upon us with the decreasing daylight and temperature. In the city they call it "cocooning". I hear it's quite trendy. In the countryside it's called "not getting soaking wet and freezing". As I get ready for winter at home, I am appalled to find that the appliances have all given each other some deadly disease. Whatever it is; its as contagious as the Winter Vomiting bug but much more dangerous because there's a strange sort of appliance health plan that makes all appliances get terminally ill at about the same time. Appliances are like light bulbs- when one goes the others are sure to follow. At last count my heating, laptop, washing machine, dryer, and CD player were all on their way to intensive care. And that's just the big collective stuff. Discmans, cameras and small electronic gadgets are the first to go. I find myself watching the television for early warning signs. Each time I boot up the computer I hold my breath. I'm considering draping strings of garlic over the stuff that still works.

I don't mean to sound like an old fogey but as a consumer I'm getting fed up with the consumer experience. Food is being made to last longer and longer, while appliances have the life expectancy of a small bug. Do we really need another neat box, covered in a see through wrapper, containing individually wrapped biscuits cleverly packaged in little snack packs of twos? That's four layers of wrapping for every biscuit. Having a coffee break is like playing pass the parcel. Then again biscuits are made to last. There's a little individually wrapped cake in the US called a Hostess Twinkie that has a shelf life of 25 years. That's about 314 months more than the average Discman. Appliances are no longer built to last. Worse of all they're not made to be fixed.

A West Cork Life

Those of an ecological bent bemoan the days when we all used to darn socks (well actually it was the days when women and bachelors without mothers used to darn socks). Now we just chuck the old ones out. But the same goes for fridges, washing machines, dryers computers, and televisions. It's not only because we're all greedy little human magpies who love shiny new things and get bored easily. It's also because no one wants to fix our broken stuff.

I can't count the times I've been told that something is not worth fixing- and being charged for that information. Computers (the most shiny and new of all our stuff) are notorious for not being worth fixing. This generally means that parts and labour will cost more than buying a new machine. That's not only because parts and labour cost a fortune but also because the newer shinier model of the same machine usually costs less than it did six months ago when you bought yours. Which is another way of saying that it's cheaper to have somebody over in Asia make you a whole new machine than to have someone over here call out to the house and fix the old one. No wonder manufacturer's guarantees are getting shorter. I used to think that a three-month guarantee was ludicrous- but how about one month? One month? You must be joking. How can a manufacturer not feel responsible if the damn thing stops working after one month? And I'm not talking about fly by night brands no one has heard of. I'm talking huge international brands with advertising budgets bigger than a developing country's export economy. There is, however, some comfort in buying well-known brands. At least you're pretty sure that the thing won't break down the day you buy it and you have a dedicated service person you can call when it inevitably does. His/her job is to tell you it isn't worth fixing.

I do have one appliance that works like a dream. Better yet when it gets a bit under the weather, I can call someone who comes to fix it. In fact when I first moved into the house this appliance hadn't worked for many years. Not a bother - it was stripped and cleaned. Its broken bits were fixed and the little fiddly bits that couldn't be fixed were replaced. It's such a comfort as it purrs away in the kitchen that we've given her a name. We call her Babe. She is a cream Aga range. The model was shiny and new over ninety years ago.

October 2002

'Tis The Pre-Season To Be Stressed Out

There's no denying it: Autumn is firmly established. In fact Winter is sneaking in most mornings, spray-painting the fields with a frost air gun. On fine days they glitter in the morning sun and dazzle your eyes - bringing on a fit of sneezing. The seasonal changes bring colds and flus as surely as the trees on the drive turn a flaming red. In Autumn my nose and my trees match. We've been happily settling into the long evenings around the fire and then just as soon as Halloween was over- its back. The Threat of Christmas looms ominously over the horizon, dangling tinsel in its jaws as it lies back on a bed of crumpled wrapping paper and laughs. Ho, ho, ho indeed.

Now don't get me wrong. I love Christmas and I am aware that it is above all a religious holiday; but go and tell that to someone who has an army of elves to do all the work. Not to mention a platinum credit card. It's hard to avoid that knot in your stomach when the postman keeps slipping toy catalogues in with the bills. Soon the Pound Shop will have a honour guard of 3 ft tall singing Santa Claus' at its door (I'm sorry but I'm going to be one of those quaint grannies that refuses to call it the EuroShop). The supermarket will be stacked with boxes of Christmas crackers from floor to ceiling and you won't be able to swing a cat on any street without hitting something that wants you to buy it for Christmas. In fact I saw a new shop that only sells Christmas sweets and decorations opening last week. They didn't even have the decency to wait until Halloween was over. As far as I'm concerned it's a question of way too much, way too early. I just hope and pray that the An Post strike will mean that I won't be receiving my very own personalised countdown to Christmas. They sent me one last November. What sadist in Dublin thought that up? Are you kidding? I need my own personalised countdown to Christmas like I need another leak in the plumbing.

A West Cork Life

Christmas may be the season to be jolly, but pre-Christmas is the season to be stressed out. This is the time of the year when I start avoiding certain women. They're lovely and kind, warm, wonderful women. But at this time of the year they change their greeting from the traditional: "Isn't it fine/lovely/miserable out today?" to: "So? All set for Christmas?" They then will proceed to list how far behind they are, finishing with: "I've nothing bought for Michael, and I haven't the mince pies made. But, thank God I got the puddings done that weekend when we had that gale - I always make them for my sisters as well- and at least I've the small fella's bikes all paid up!" I smile wanly and throw up my hands. What was I doing that wet, wet, weekend? I was probably watching re-runs on TV. Guilt rears its ugly head. It will stay there until 3am on Christmas morning when I collapse after my traditional last minute wrapping of the last minute presents. I'm lucky in that I do have some defences against the unrelenting pressure to get into the Christmas spirit. Even thinking about Christmas is forbidden until after Thanksgiving that falls at the end of November. We then must restrain from any action until December 8th. Before I moved to West Cork, the 8th was etched in my memory as a day one processed around my boarding school in a white veil, belting out "Ora Pronobis" like a football hooligan; while waving candles and lilies about, trying not to singe the veil of the girl in front of you. Now it means 10% day and the signal to start the present-buying frenzy. However, not a holly leaf is put up in the house until after my birthday. It falls conveniently ten days before Christmas. It's as good an excuse as any to stop small children from going into hyperactive overdrive too early. Anyway, I hate sharing the spotlight with a major holiday.

The gales are back. It starts with a whistle. If the TV or stereo is on too loud you wouldn't notice it, but about an hour later you can't hear yourself think. Outside bits of paper, branches, and the occasional small mammal flies by the window. Trees are flailing about in an alarming manner and I reassure myself that any tree that was going to come down did so during the Christmas hurricane when we lost seven big pines along the drive. Gales generally last for either a day or three days and they blow from the southwest. The weird thing is that when the eye of the storm passes overhead, everything becomes deathly still. It is so disconcerting that it wakes me in the middle of the night and I lie there, snuggling under the pile of duvets, and have to wait for it to pick up again before I can go back to sleep.

November 2002

"If I Were You, I Wouldn't Start From Here"

Living in rural West Cork, you get pretty good at giving directions. Learning to give precise directions is important otherwise my visitors end up driving around and around for hours, passing Balineen once every few goes until they are rescued by an understanding native. West Cork roads are sneaky. A road can wind along a full 360 degrees without you noticing. When you first move here, you're continually lost - not to mention confused. In my first year in the village, no matter which point of the compass I was headed, if I got lost I would eventually end up in Lyre. That's the way the roads go around here. In fact I might end up several times in Lyre even though each time I'd head off in the opposite direction. The magical thing about West Cork roads is the way they can bring you back exactly where you started from. In a spirit of adventure worthy of the great 19th century explorers, I once drove off from Timoleague in an attempt to navigate the ultimate back road home. After driving for 15 minutes I arrived right smack back in front of Charlie Madden's pub where I'd been parked. Thankfully you do get better at it after a while. West Cork will turn you into a homing pigeon in a couple of years. It's a survival skill. If you don't acquire that boreen sixth sense, you could disappear altogether:

"Where'd Tina go? I haven't seen her in ages."

"I don't know, last time I saw her she said she was taking the back road to Macroom!"

I've heard that if you're very lost it's the fault of the faeries. It seems that they love tricking people. You must get out of the car, turn your jacket inside out and put it back on again. Apparently the faeries find this so hilarious that they let you off. Of course, if you don't believe in that sort of thing you could always just ask for directions. Mind you, in West Cork that can almost be as fanciful as asking the faeries.

The funny thing about asking for directions

is that people in West Cork love to oblige, but they'll always first answer with a shake of the head that indicates that they haven't a clue where you want to go. After a few shakes, your guide will scratch the back of his neck with a look of intense concentration. Then he'll bend down into the window and whisper in a conspiratory tone: "Well now- If I were you, I wouldn't start from here." This is actually a highly philosophical statement. A conundrum such as determining how many angels can dance on a pin head is as easy as counting how many cows there are in a field compared to a statement like: "If I were you, I wouldn't start from here." I'm sure that many of us would like not to be where we are when we set off to go somewhere-but we'd never envisioned the possibility of it being otherwise. What it actually means is that you are, indeed, very lost. You are so lost, in fact, that you need directions to get to a place where you can start to go to wherever it was that you wanted to go to. However, the prospect of not starting where you are can be somewhat daunting for someone used to: "Take the first left and turn right at the traffic lights."

The actual giving of directions can become a saga of biblical proportions. This is mainly because it is important for people to tell you which way you shouldn't go and there are a lot more ways not to go somewhere than there are ways to get there. People giving directions in West Cork take great pains to tell you in minute detail all the roads you shouldn't take. They carefully describe landmarks you must totally ignore. "You'll come up to a road that goes over a bridge and turns to the right before passing the church- you know the one? Take no notice!"

When calling on the telephone for directions the motto is: be prepared. You'll need at least two sheets of A4 paper and a good pencil as you'll have to write down a journey worthy of Ulysses. Details will include interesting geological features, well placed pubs, and treacherous bends in the road. I have often found myself driving slowly up a boreen trying to make sense of cryptic scribbles: "Take left at the rusty gate (red cloth). Windey bit about a mile, Turn left at daffodils."

I remember one of the first times I took directions on the phone. I was going to visit someone down past Skibbereen. The directions included looking out for a milk churn. They led me away from the main road down a tiny boreen that wound itself towards the sea. I read; "Turn left at the Ginger Cat." I had written down the directions without a second thought, imagining that the Ginger Cat was a pub. The road climbed through a bleak landscape offset by the slate sea and lead sky. Up ahead I could see a tiny blue and white cottage that stuck out like a Christmas cake on the grey scenery. That must be it, I thought, scanning the building for a Murphy's sign. Then as I came alongside the cottage, I saw a huge ginger cat sitting on the wall. Sure enough, after the cat was a little boreen to the left. I swear that cat winked as I drove by.

November 2002

Winter Solstice

The dark days are upon us. By 3 o'clock in what used to be the afternoon, the back hall has faded into the shadows. This means it feels like you're doing laundry in the middle of the night. The up side is that you can't possibly do anything like sweeping or cleaning out the cobwebs as you can't see them. Adding to the darkness are the regular power cuts that come with the gales. It's humbling to find that all those really important things you had planned to do in the evening (including writing this column) must be put on hold. Thanks to Babe the Aga, and a good open fire, we can still get on with the truly essential things like keeping warm and eating. The urgency of doing anything else just fades into the soft candlelight and quiet conversation with the whistle of the wind as our only background music.

Soon, by the time the kids get home from school the lights will be on and the fire lit. Feeding the dogs, bringing in the coal, or doing anything that demands going outside must be done before 3:30pm or you can go at it with a flashlight - not an easy task when there's a 60-mph wind gutting the garage.

In the dark despair of these days like nights I find solace that the worst is almost over. In two weeks it's December 21: Winter Solstice. There's another three weeks of darkness after the Solstice (which we won't notice because it's Christmas and the pub is always dark anyway)- then we'll feel the change. The days will slowly but surely get longer until one morning I'll see the sharp green stalks sticking out of the black earth and I'll know that its over. Another ten days after that and the daffodils will be lining the drive. Redemption.

In 2000 we marked the Winter Solstice in the village by officially opening the NS's Millennium Park which was a very appropriate date as the park consisted of four monuments which recreated ancient sites found in our area.

A tall Gullane or standing stone, a Dolmen, a bee-hive hut, and a round tower now grace the four corners of the school pitch. A pageant was performed in the grey cold day and most of the village turned out for the event. After freezing in the cold wind, with our toes chilled by the wet gloopy mud of the pitch, we all gathered back in the old school hall for speeches and teas.

Our guest of honour remembered his schooldays: "When I was a child attending the National School in this very hall, we also had a park of sorts. It was a bamboo garden," he said. I immediately listened up. I had always been intrigued by a thick hedge of bamboo growing along a field near the old school building. It always seemed a bit incongruous waving about in the wind and I'd always wondered what chance planting had encouraged an entire hedge of bamboo to grow in the middle of nowhere. I had even taken some cuttings in the hope that I too could have a long line of bamboo in the front field. They had, however, always failed to take root.

"We would cut down the long canes and line them up against the fire to dry. They were a reminder of what we had coming to us if we did not behave."

Many in the hall laughed and nodded

their heads, remembering. I tired to remain interested yet blank as the truth of the bamboo sunk in. Having never attended a school where corporal punishment was acceptable, it came as something of a shock.

"I also remember that the floors had knot holes in the wood and when the Master left us on our own we would take the bamboo canes and throw them down the holes. The poor Master would be demented trying to figure out where we had hidden them, but he never did find out. I am happy to say that we now live in more enlightened times and we believe that children should be happy in school."

As applause rippled around the hall, I thought of the piles of bamboo canes lying under the floor boards. And I was glad that my children where going to school in more enlightened times than in the dark days when the threat of the cane was common. But I never did look at that bamboo hedge in quite the same way. And I'm damn glad it never took in my garden.

December 2002

I'm Dreaming Of A White Christmas

Damn but it's cold! I know I sound like a broken record but I can't help it. I repeat it at every chance meeting, every chat on the phone, every call to the door. Hell -I even go around mumbling it under my breath, puffing little smoke signals as I go. So I'm committing it to print- It's damn cold! Keeping the house warm in winter is like trying to heat up a fridge from the inside out. We take turns hogging the fire as we watch telly at night; toasting first one side then the other. The duvets are piled so high that I have to burrow out of bed every morning and carry out archaeological digs to find my daughters and wake them.

By the by, I take back every thing I've ever said about having resolved the mouse problem by having three cats. My entire theory has crumbled in the cold snap. There are effectively no mice downstairs. The kitchen is pristine. The pantry is untouched. That's because the cats have sensibly decided to stay asleep on the Aga for the duration of the cold spell. The mice must have figured it out and so have moved upstairs. The lack of anything edible hasn't seemed to deter them. I think they've taken up residence in the skirting board behind the hot press, which must be like a package winter break to the Canaries for a mouse. So, along with the hot water bottle, we now each carry a cat up when retiring for the night. Unfortunately the cats seem to think that the mountains of duvets are for them and are not at all bothered by the little scutterings under the floorboards. Still I figure that no mouse is going to climb into bed with me if I have a cat asleep on my head.

And so this is Christmas, as the song goes. Having successfully navigated the "Pre-Season to be Stressed Out" without so much as buying one string of tinsel, I am now ready to plunge into Christmas and enjoy it. If you've been clever like me, and you didn't fall for all the pre-season hype, you can truly start to get into the spirit right about now. You don't want to peak too early. Sometime around 11:30 pm on Christmas Day the festive season will hit its apogee. If you pace yourself correctly, it will stay on a steady course, needing only a push here, a day off there; to slide gracefully to the final climax on Woman's Christmas. I want to make sure I'll be there with bells on - though I'd go in a wheel chair hooked up to a drip rather than miss the night.

I've decided to have myself a merry little Christmas. And where I live, when you're looking to enjoy yourself and forget all your cares (not to mention keeping warm), you go to town and head for the pub. It has never let me down, but at Christmas it throbs with good-times energy. I remember one Christmas sitting next to my friend Sheila and commenting on the miraculous way Christmas lifts our spirits. She raised a glass and said: "We have Christmas because we need it. Merry Christmas, darling." We clinked our glasses, looked at the happy faces, and gave each other the first of many Christmas rounds of hugs.

Christmas in the back of beyond is a bacchanal. We glut on food and drink, and good company, and song and dance. We huddle around fires and tell stories. We laugh until we weep. We sing out until our hearts feel that they will break; while outside the wind howls and the darkness reigns, and we find comfort in the fact that we have each other. We embrace people we wouldn't drink with in the spring, and buy drinks for those we merely nod to in the summer. We drink, we eat and we are merry. And thank God for that.

I'm hoping the cold will serve to make this Christmas perfect. Nothing quite does it for me to get that "Joy To The World" glow than to wake up on Christmas morning and find the fields covered in a blanket of white. Even an icing sugar dusting of snow gets my heart beating to the tune of "Jingle Bells". It snowed last two years ago. It was Christmas Eve and the dogs started howling strangely. It wasn't the forceful, joyous howling they do at the moon. This was a plaintive almost inquisitive howl. I don't remember who saw it first but soon a cry went up and we were all baying with the dogs: " Its snowing! It's snowing! It's snowing!" We ran out and danced around in it. The dogs jumped about, snapping their jaws as they tried to eat the snowflakes. Even the cats joined us. We got a torch and made huge spirals over the front field, turning the night into a spray of gold glitter falling on our heads. For days I had been unconsciously wishing for snow in that silent whisper that hopes Santa will bring you a bike. And I got my wish. So I figure, if we all wish really hard, we're sure to get it to snow again. Give it a go. Wish for snow. Who knows? We might just make it happen.

Merry Christmas.

December 2002

Imbolc: Did St. Bridgit Detox?

OK. I confess. I too got suckered in. What can you do? It's that time. I'm not stupid, and I'm certainly old enough to know better, but off I go with hope in my heart for a healthier tomorrow. Armed with three grapefruits, some low fat soya milk, and a copy of "The Easy Way to Stop Smoking" I am ready to face 2003.

It is almost the lovely holiday of Imbolc, or St Bridgid's day. February 2 used to herald the coming of Spring, crosses made out of rushes, and spectacular rainbows. These days the season is largely dedicated to getting healthy (and slim). It's as if St.Bridgid has become the patron Saint of detox. What is it about January that makes us all want to better ourselves at the same time? It seems as if the entire Western world is obsessed every year with the double ds of diet and detox? If the coverage in the newspapers and magazines are anything to go by, we are far more worried about losing weight and getting healthy than about the possibility of war between the US and Iraq. North Korea is a mere blip compared with our concerns about cholesterol. Are we mad or what? Why do it now? Why do it together?

Some may think it has to do with the overindulgence of the festive season. That's just misplaced guilt. I know I ate more Belgian chocolates in the last month than during the entire preceding year. But frankly, so what? Stuffing your face in the deep mid-winter is traditional. It made sense. The cattle could not be fed over the winter, and the veg would rot so you just ate everything in sight before it went off. We were also stocking up for the coldest months. In the dark, dark "days" of mid winter our bodies demand that we stuff our faces and put on protective layers of fat to combat the cold. Then we are meant to digest for about a month or two. I came out of Christmas stuffed and contented and wanted nothing more than to sleep until Spring. Judging from the amounts of loud yawning around me I'd say most of you feel the same. And so you should- it's the natural rhythm of the season. Let's face it, our ancestors lived in caves. We weren't meant to go jogging in January. We were meant to be sleeping as we digest the rich food we had over Christmas. Late winter is really not meant to be for anything more energetic than scooting over to root out the remote from under the duvet. So why in God's name do we pick the first week of January to shape up and clean out? It is not about guilt. It's blatant manipulation.

You see the minute the last flute of champagne is imbibed at the stroke of midnight is not only the cue to ring in the New Year. It's also when headlines around the Western world start promoting the idea that we need to get healthy (and slim) RIGHT HERE RIGHT NOW. The barrage of "get healthy (and slim)" messages makes us do this silly, not to mention delusional, dance with our minds. We imagine we will rise from the bloated, pasty-faced ashes of our former selves (like the happy svelte, phoenixes that we really are) sometime in June if only we start RIGHT NOW. It's stupid. They do it to us again around May. At least the frenzy to get into shape in JUST EIGHT WEEKS makes sense in May. After all, it's likely that in about eight weeks you may be exposing bits of your body that haven't seen the light of day for six months. The threat of swimwear is a reasonable incentive to diet. But this January obsession makes no sense at all. I've got months of big wooly jumpers ahead of me before I'll be seen in a long sleeved T-shirt.

Having in my day experimented with everything from the blood-type diet (very interesting) to the cabbage soup diet (really boring and unsociable due to the lingering smell of cabbage soup in the house and the propensity for building up wind), I have some advice. Shooting from the ample hip- here goes:

1. If you want to loose weight: eat less and move more.

2. If you're going for healthy: eat less fat, more fresh food, cut out processed/refined anything. Don't smoke. Don't drink. Take up a sport. You'll probably loose weight as well.

3. Forget all of the above until about May. This is a terrible time to do anything but sleep. Wait another few weeks. Already the change in daylight is becoming apparent. Remember the Golden Rule of Dieting: never diet if it still gets dark before six.

4. To help with the January get-fit guilt: buy some fruit, some low fat products, and a self-help book and take to the bed until Spring. That's what I do.

January 2003

Forget Venus and Mars on Valentine's Day

At least three different Saint Valentine, all of them martyrs, are mentioned in the early martyrologies with a feast day on February 14. There are a number of explanations as to why this date, and St Valentine himself, have become the Hunka-Hunka Burnin' Holiday of Lurve we have today. Some believe that the origins date from the time when it was commonly believed that February 14 (i.e. half way through the second month of the year) was when the birds began to pair. Some experts state that it originated with St. Valentine, a Roman priest who was martyred for refusing to give up Christianity. He died on February 14,

A West Cork Life

269 AD, the same day that had been devoted to love lotteries: Girls and boys would pull names from a jar and pair up for the duration of the festival of Lupercalia. This custom of pulling names in a lottery continued throughout the Middle Ages, when young men and women drew names from a bowl to see who their valentines would be. They would wear these names on their sleeves for one week, hence giving rise to the expression "to wear your heart on your sleeve" (as well as inspiring a hit single a thousand years later in 1976- give or take a century.).

Legend also has it that the martyred St Valentine left a farewell note for his jailer's daughter, and signed it "From Your Valentine". Other stories state that the priest married lovers while in jail. In 496 AD Pope Gelasius set aside February 14 to honor St. Valentine. Over time, February 14 became the date for exchanging love messages and St. Valentine became the patron saint of lovers. It is from such humble beginnings that the commercial Hearts&Flowers/ Love&Kisses runaway holiday success we have today emerged.

Then again relationships between men and women have also evolved dramatically since the days when Victorians enjoyed the first mass-produced Valentine's cards. These usually depicted a brave, dashing gentlemen telling a shy, blushing maiden not to worry her pretty little head about anything too taxing for her tiny brain. In fact one way to experience how much things have changed (if you're a guy) is to walk up to a girl at the bar and try that out as a chat up line. My advice is to say it fast and run. No siree, today's lovers enjoy a relationship between equals.

Except, that is, on Valentine's Day.

Ironically this is the one holiday where gender parity has not been achieved. It's a shocking thing for a feminist to admit, but it's true- the onus is on the guys to produce the goods. Let's face it, women can get away with a card. In fact a big smoochie Happy Valentines Day kiss and a pint will make a guy very happy. It doesn't work both ways. Men - especially those in a long-term relationship- know it. There are rules: You must get something special for your partner on Valentine's Day. It has to be more special than whatever she gets you. Forgetting is not an option. Which is why so many men start getting panicky on February 13. I hear the sale of anti-acid tablets shoots up in mid-February. The day before Valentine's Day newsagents and novelty gift shops are full of men wandering around looking confused. They are generally in their work clothes- which is a dead give-away that they'd totally forgotten to get something until the last minute. They stare in wonder at giant cards festooned with teddy bears and hearts. Their faces frown in concentration as they try to remember which ones are the special chocolates she likes. Does she eat chocolates? Is she on a diet? Does it matter? Sweat beads on their brow as they try and figure out what is the right thing to buy. You can understand their concern. The choices generally include a three-foot tall teddy bear. Is this an appropriate gift for an equal? Will a working mother of four who does Yoga once a week appreciate a cuddly toy the size of an overweight toddler? Then again something is telling them that it might just work. It's a tricky situation.

One thing is certain: the stuffed bear is better than no gift at all. Unless, of course, you want to recreate the St Valentine's Day Massacre (no bonus points for guessing who's going to be lined up against the wall). Forget Venus and Mars. On St Valentines Day, Men are from "What the hell am I going to get her?' and Women are from "You'd better not forget".

February 2003

Nesting Instincts

Well I can't say I'm sorry that February is over. It isn't as bad as January, when the lack of sunshine and warmth has me practically catatonic, but it's still pretty awful. It's cold. It's wet. It's windy. Every move outside is a battle. Even breathing demands your full attention when you get hit in the face with a 60mph gust of icy sleet. Each trip into town first requires a Herculean feat of strength as you battle the elements for possession of the car door. The kitchen door spent most of last month tied to the Aga with an old pair of ballet tights to avoid it flying off its hinges. This is the time of year when I wonder what possessed me to choose West Cork over the Carribean. Lenny Henry, the comedian, once described Ireland as a "cold Jamaica". In February the operative word is "cold" (And wet, and windy, he might have added.) But just when I think I can't take another gale, or another school run in the dark- the day gets longer, the light changes, a rainbow appears and yes- early flowers bloom. With a wink and a nod, the countryside flirts with the idea of Spring and the seduction begins again.

Not that I'm heaving a big sigh of relief quite yet. We've still a few cold, wet, windy months to go-but as I watch the first daffodils being whacked senseless by a hailstorm, their yellow heads snapping back and forth like demented teenagers moshing at their first gig, I do feel a faint smile creeping up. It's not over yet but the end is in sight.

This time of the year doesn't have a lot going for it- the pubs are near empty, everyone's broke (hence the empty pub), and it's cold. (And wet. And windy.) There are, however, a few small blessings to keep us going until April. The Camelia bush is in full bloom again. It's definitely the Mad Lula of the garden. And when the sun does shine the rainbows are so spectacular that they put a Hollywood FX's department to shame. Shuddering miserably as a cold mixture of sleet and mushy rain drenched my frozen frame last Sunday, I looked up to see the most beautiful, most perfect, double rainbow ever seen (Just believe me. You had to be there.) It knocked the socks off the reigning champ, which was a double rainbow I saw once while driving to Tralee.

The heavens are definitely worth watching at this time of the year: If you bother to look up, you'll see rainbows, clouds the size of cathedrals, and the occasional hawk all dashing above your head. Actually, the birds have all gone mental. They presumably respond to the extra hours of sunlight by getting the house building bug in a big way. They're all at it. They spin madly overhead as they try to fly against the wind; most of them carrying building materials. The crows seem to spend their days going back and forth to Sticks'R Us to pick up supplies. The skies are full of crows bumping into each other like Sunday shoppers in a DIY superstore.

Last week I came home from town in a raging gale. I had just managed to maneuver myself out the car without having my shoulder ripped off at the socket, when something caught my eye. Sitting perfectly still in the middle of the yard, as dust devils and leaves and bits of rubbish swirled around, was a little nest. It was exquisitely round, and green, and snug.

It would probably cost millions in consultants' fees to come up with something as well made, as perfectly packaged, and as inviting, as this little nest.

It fits easily into the palm of my hand. It's cosy and warm and very beautiful. The main components are tiny twigs, pine needles and moss. Threaded through these natural building blocks are manmade materials. As I sat warming myself on the Aga and examined it, I felt a lump catch in my throat.

The bird that had worked so diligently had inadvertently woven our household history into this little masterpiece. Here was some blue embroidery thread I remembered. There was some bailer twine wrapped around what looked like a bit of fishing line from last summer. A number of similar looking plastic threads had me stumped until I realised that they had been carefully picked out of the empty coal bags that litter the garage. Tucked in with the moss were the dog hairs and dust dinosaurs that I regularly sweep out the door. There were also big chunks of lint from the dryer (One bird's lint is another bird's insulation). And best of all, threaded delicately through the intricate pattern of green moss, twigs, and coal sack threads, was a single strand of silver tinsel from our Christmas tree.

March 2003

The Woods Are Alive with the Sound of Midgets

Welcome back sunshine! All is forgiven! (Where the hell have you been? I suspect Lanzarote.) Like an ice cube on a hot day, my lethargy and despair just melted away as the sun finally shone. Judging from the rampant conviviality that ran amok through West Cork this weekend -so has everyone else's. We hugged greetings like long lost friends and invited each other over for a picnic/BBQ/water fight. Reclaiming our true personalities from the clutches of an awful winter, we delighted in each other's company again. The return of the prodigal sun made us rediscover why we love living here so much. It's like waking from a deep coma and realising with huge relief that you're still alive and it's a beautiful day. I take this opportunity to apologise for that drippy grey woman who dragged herself around complaining about everything only weeks ago. That wasn't me. That was my depressed twin.

The general state of unbridled happiness was not lost on the animals. The birds sang so loud that they managed to drown out the sound of strimmers and chainsaws last weekend. The dogs spent the days tearing around chasing each other for ten minute rounds, then they'd roll over and play dead in the sun for three hours. Lambs frolicked in the fields, foals pranced around, and I saw a terrier clearly overcome by the joy of it all. Is there anything more comical than an amorous terrier whose object of desire is ever so slightly bigger than himself?

The landscape has jollied up as well, moving through the colour chart towards the happy yellows. The gorse is blooming, the daffs are still soldiering on, but they've been beaten hands down this year by the primroses bursting from ever nook and cranny. The fields have shifted to Kelly green which is a heinous colour for a jumper, but just perfect on a rolling field at sunset when "everything turns to gold" (Thanks John Spillane!).

There are other signs that the season has changed. I spotted a fly in the kitchen. Outside the lazy drone of the bumblebees and other buzzing bugs can be heard in the rare moments of silence between the strimmers and the birds. People always think that the countryside is quiet but it's actually very noisy. It's just a different quality of noise.

Swarms of midges hover around ready to overpower the first unsuspecting head that moves in their vicinity. When the girls were little they used to call them midgets (As in: "Mum, the woods are full of midgets!"). I like the mispronunciation. It makes me think of really tiny but very ferocious flying people that buzz around in packs like miniature football fans after a match. I jest, but I actually have a lot of respect for them. I learned the hard way. It was at a BBQ years ago, down in Durrus. The beautiful evening was marred by midges. I decided to ignore them. It was a mind over matter thing. I was going to pretend they weren't buzzing around my head. I figured that I'd rather have an itch or two the next day, than spend the evening wrapped in a burka swatting midges. Everything went fine. The midges feasted and I pretended they didn't exist. We all had lovely time. I woke up at 2am with my head on fire. I now suspect that if one of them actually did get up your nose, it could fry your brain.

At the house we celebrated the return of sunlight by drinking a few colds ones in the front field at sunset. We also had an impromtu music session outside, visited friends and climbed some trees. Through it all the sun shone with real heat. Which was a good thing because the water pump broke down on Saturday. Had that happened a month ago I probably would have collapsed in a sad heap by the fire, but with the sun beating down we happily went into "Little House on the Prairie" mode. We learnt how to live without running water the Christmas we had the hurricane. We were without power or water for a week. The first thing you do is to gather all the containers you can find. If you're a proper blow-in you will have some big fermenting bins stuck in a shed somewhere. Then you pop over to a neighbour (or the Wheel of Fortune in town if the whole village is out) and fill'er up. While you're at your neighbour's you take a quick shower. In the sunshine it almost seems like an adventure again.

Of course, behind our delighted smiles lurks THE FEAR. Will it last? Will we have a summer this year? Is this as good at it's going to get? Who cares? Just soak up some rays and bathe in the warmth of it all. Right here, right now.

Tina Pisco
Not to worry. We'll think about that in July. It's just a question of mind of matter.

April 2003

Pisco's Corollary and the Joys of Spring

We're back on track folks! Like a lover who arrives on the doorstep with a really big bunch of flowers and a goofy smile, West Cork has a way of re-seducing me every Spring no matter how badly I've been treated the previous winter.

To mark the occasion the front field has had an aerial squad ducking and diving for the past two days. The swallow advance party flew in on Friday. It wasn't just the swallows that made their re-appearance over the Easter weekend. The tourists are back as well. I know we're meant to be in for hard times but I couldn't get a room in a B&B/hotel/hostel in West Cork last

Saturday night. The Celtic Tiger may be dead but her cubs are still spending their disposal income down on the Irish Riviera (along with a large proportion of Spain's youth, if the pubs are anything to go by). And do we produce the goods? We most certainly do. The sun is shining. The surf's up. The fields are full of Disney cartoon bunnies and lambs and calves and foals. Primroses line every bend in the road with frilly yellow flowers. The pubs are jammers. The sheer beauty of it all is infectious.

So armed with reserves of energy that I haven't had for months, I go into high gear. It's time for the Big Sweep. Before you can actually yield a broom, however, you need to wade through piles and piles of stuff- let's call it junk- that has accumulated over the winter. It's like a grisly housekeeping version of triage. Junk accumulates at an astronomical rate in the house.

In 1958 Prof. Cyril Northcote Parkinson devised what he modestly called Parkinson's Law. It states that work expands so as to fill the time available for its completion. In other words jobs expand to fit the time allotted to them. (He came to his conclusions after studying over-staffing in the British Civil Service. Happy days.) I find this to be particularly true of homework and freelance writing deadlines. There is a parallel that applies to old stone houses. I modestly call it Pisco's Corrollary: It states that Junk willl accumulate to fill all the available spaces in a country house and then some. If you have sheds they will not only fill up with your junk, but everyone else's as well. The same applies to large yards.

As I write, I'm looking at a little plastic tub that contains plastic beads that has taken up residence on my windowsill for several years. How did it get there? Whose is it? Does anybody want it? Could anybody I know use a little plastic tub full of beads? Can I throw it out? Throwing it out is the last resort. Finding it a new home or recycling it are the top choices. Every charity shop in the area gets a visit as I stumble in with boxes of clothes, shoes, toys, books and odds and ends. I am generous with my junk. Like a second hand Lady Bountiful I donate boxes to anybody who'll take'em. I recycle with a vengeance. I gather up bottles, paper, cardboard, and go back and forth to town with the boot rattling.

But no matter how much triage I process there's always some junk left over. In the past I would order a big skip and chuck it all out. Mea Culpa. Had I let the junk just pile up we would be sequestered by now. We would not be able to reach the door, much less open it. The sheer volume of little plastic things that hide in cereal packets would have swallowed us up. But since the cost of hiring a big skip has jumped to the level of a really nice weekend break for two that I can't afford, I have a real problem on my hands. So far I've come up with burning it or turning it into an art installation entitled Leftover Junk. Do send any suggestions on a postcard.

Finally, here is a joke I received this week. I think it's a contender for the perfect West Cork joke. That it was sent to me by a gentleman who lives in Cincinnati and who has only visited here for a few days only makes it worthier:

Father O'Mahoney answers the phone:
"Hello, is this Father O'Mahoney?"
"It is"
"This is the Revenue Commissioners. Can you help us?"
"I'll try"
"Do you know a Ted Houlihan?"
"I do"
"Is he a member of your congregation?"
"He is"
"Did he donate £10,000 to the church?"
"He will".

April 2003

Surviving the Plumbing Nightmare

Thank God for the blue bells. I really needed them last week. They appeared, as usual, overnight but this year they have gone all out to steal the spotlight from the primroses. There is nothing quite as beautiful as the lilac haze that carpets our woods and paints every nook and cranny along the boreens with a surreal glow. At this time of year the forty shades of green compete with a riot of hues of which the bluebells are the most riotous. Pink, deep purple, pale yellow and fragile white flowers dot the fields in a kaleidoscope of colour. May made a spectacular entrance and was welcomed by all-though some of us needed the lift in spirits more than others. We all have our hidden fears. Living in an old house I have a few. Last week one of the worst became a reality.

Anyone who has ever laid awake worrying about the gurgling in the pipes knows the feeling. It was seven o'clock on a bleak, grey morning. I woke with a thumping heart and panic gripping my soul. A gale was raging outside, turning the view from my bedroom window into a scene normally only glimpsed from the inside of a washing machine. Water slashed against the panes, water whipped around the stone walls, water rumbled through the gutters, water hammered above my head. Above my head? It only took a spilt second to differentiate between the screeching wind, the lashing rain and another, totally different, gushing noise. My brain screamed that it was just a dream. This wasn't really happening- but it was. I had woken up to my worst plumbing nightmare. It sounded as if someone had turned on a high-pressure hose in the attic. There was water everywhere. The light fixtures had evolved into free flowing taps. The plasterboard was sagging. The noise was deafening.

In the ten minutes that it took to determine the cause (a ball cock had gone in a water tank in the attic) and dash out to the shed to turn off the pump, the flood had coursed through two floors. At first I hesitated to run barefoot into the gale until I realised that I was already soaked. Sure it was raining outside- but it was also raining in the kitchen. Those ten minutes felt like three hours as we went into heroic high gear. I kept getting flashbacks of every water disaster movie I've ever seen, from the Poseidon Adventure to Titanic (though The Money Pit would have been more appropriate). Kate Winslet has nothing on me. I want a medal. I have faced my fears and have survived and I have a gaping hole in the ceiling to prove it.

We now face weeks of cleaning up, builders, and plaster dust tracking our footprints through the house. Not to mention insurance assessors. What is it about officials (Gardai, tax inspectors, customs officers) that make the most innocent Saint amongst us feel like a psychopathic serial killer with a secret criminal record and bodies buried in the back field? I must say that the assessor who came out to view the damage was lovely and made every effort to put me at ease. I still felt uncomfortable though one can hardly be accused of exaggerating a claim when you have a great view of the rafters where the ceiling used to be. Family and friends have suggested that this disaster was a sign, a message from Above (no kidding). They're probably right. I just have to figure out whether it means that we should move, or whether we should put in a mezzanine.

Someone once said that America and Britain were two countries separated by a common language. They obviously had never visited these shores. West Cork English has a way of making subtle statements that are all about the sub-text. A skilful use of the word after, for example, determines how long it's been since the event took place. "He's after leaving" means that the person in question is definitely gone. "He's just after leaving" means that you can still catch up with him in the car park. Repetition is also an important cue. When chatting on the phone, or leaving a place, only those with time on their hands say Good bye just the once. The number of "byes" increases with the need for speed. In the village it is customary to say five when really pressed for time as in: "Bye, bye, bye, bye, bye."

Standing in the queue at the ATM the other day I overheard two women chatting and it occurred to me that before I moved to West Cork I wouldn't have understood what they meant:

"Are you coming in or going out?" asked the

first one.

"I'm in between really" replied the second. It made perfect sense. If you don't get it you haven't lived here long enough.

May 2003

Happy Anniversary

You may not have noticed it but this column marks an anniversary. It's been a year that the West Cork Advertiser has been gracing your kitchen table (and, if you're like me, lining your cat litter. It's the perfect size.). Yes folks, I've been rambling, ranting and raving for 12 months. To paraphrase Cork songwriter John Spillane- we've traveled all around the sun, and its taken us one whole year- Well done everyone!

As I read over a year in A West Cork Life, the first thing that strikes me is that the weather really got to me. In the Spring of 2002 I was looking forward to Sponataneous BBQ's, long

A West Cork Life

lazy days on the beach, and pleasant evenings in the beer garden; but by the time the summer hit its peak I was screaming "Enough with the rain already!" A few short weeks of sun towards the end is all we got to remind us of what we'd missed. Then the cold hit. Once Autumn set in, it seems like I complained about the cold in every single column. I apologise for my continual comments about duvets and hot water bottles but, then again, as I wrote back in December trying to keep an big old stone house warm is like trying to heat a fridge from the inside out. In his travel book on the West Cork coast, Peter-Sommerville Large, described the "soft yet harsh climate which can induce lethargy and despair". He knew what he was talking about. By January 2003 the lethargy had me curled up under a pile of duvets despairing that the sun would ever shine again.

It didn't help that this was the year everybody decided to visit. 2002 will go down in our history as the Year of the Visitor. From May to October the house was teeming with parents, siblings, nieces, nephews, cousins, second cousins, their spouses, their children, my children and all their friends. Most of them didn't drive. All of them complained about the weather. Looking at a crowded photograph from that time I can count 17 people sitting down for dinner.

I showed it to one of the girls who asked me who had taken the picture? It took us a few minutes to figure out that it must have been one of the French students who also lived with us last summer. It was a great relief (and a bit of a surprise) to get a card at Christmas saying how much she'd enjoyed her stay. The poor dear passed largely unnoticed in the family fray.

I seem to have found plenty to complain about besides the weather and Nervous Visitors. Vermin figure prominently: mice, spiders, and slugs creep and crawl through the pages. I have yet to write a column on head lice. I'll get to it eventually. Every machine I own also seemed to have broken down. Cars, CD players, laptops, and washing machines, all gave up the ghost this year. Actually, as I write I'm waiting for the repairman to fix the brand new washing machine I bought to replace the one that died. It never ends.

Good stuff happened too. The World Cup was a hoot. Christmas was all it was meant to be once we'd gotten over the pre-season to be stressed out. Even January had its moments with some great Saturday afternoons in the pub. Best of all were the little things that make West Cork the only place I want to hang my hat. The kindness of neighbors, the comfort of friends, and the small triumphs of children; all wrapped up in a green and lush package that can pull me straight out of the doldrums with a single (or better yet, double) rainbow.

I was in Dublin last week at an international conference. The foreign delegates all marveled at how friendly people were. "Everyone smiles a lot here," they exclaimed, looking puzzled. I told them that if they thought Dublin was friendly they should check out West Cork. I then waxed lyrical about the daffs in my front field, the foxes peeking around the hedges, the beauty of our beaches, the great craic of our music sessions and watched them shake their heads in wonder and disbelief. "You're very lucky," they said. "Yes, I most certainly am," I replied smugly.

I thought it would be disloyal to mention that next January I'm booking off to Lanzarote.

May 2003

THE EARLY YEARS

1993-1994ish

These first appeared in the then Cork Examiner under the name of Patsy Trench.

Chaos Management

Passing in front of a large Cork bookstore I recently noticed that much space was devoted to a number of books on the same theme: "Chaos Theory". Likewise the world media have been making a big deal about "Chaos Management" as the ultimate answer to life the universe and everything. Chaos Management is new? I figure the whole theory was concocted by bunch of guys who never stopped to wonder how the shirt they last saw in a crumpled heap on the floor, magically transmutated into a clean and pressed garment hanging in the closet Ask any mother and she will tell you that her great-grandmother knew that managing chaos is the bottom line -Especially if your brood includes a two-year old. If you're like me, and you have both a two-year old AND a thirteen-year old under the same roof, then Chaos Rules. Take last Sunday evening.

Returning from a quick trip to the shop I walked into the lounge only to find that the room I'd left in a vague imitation of tidiness has been trashed in a manner worthy of the most hardcore heavy metal band.

Not one, but two cereal packets lie discarded on the floor along with an assortment of bowls, sweet wrappings, and milk bottles. Peeking from under the sofa I spy two sticky spoons that are dangerously close to sinking into oblivion. Clothes, (size 5), shoes, and one sock (the second one always runs away at the first chance) are piled on the floor. A decorative mix of crayons mingles with an array of Barbie stiletto heels - all fuschia pink and none matching. The Sunday paper, which I haven't read yet, is ripped to shreds and strewn across the carpet forming an interesting collage with the desecrated remains of an entire box of jam rings. Each biscuit has been carefully split apart and scraped of all traces of jam. Thank God for small mercies. That means they won't stick to the newspaper. Daughters #2 and 3 are lounging on the floor wrapped up in their duvets. They are watching "Mary Poppins" for the 163rd time. Daughter #4 is sitting happily amid the shredded newspaper, her angelic face covered in jam. Daughter #1, who was left in charge, is on the phone. As I turn to yell at her I notice that #4's tongue and hands are a frightening shade of blue. Under her chubby toddler toes I find the culprit. Not content with the non-toxic washable markers I so diligently buy for the kids, she has armed herself with an alcohol based 100% indelible weapon of doom instead. This marker has the notice "WILL MARK ALMOST ANY SURFACE IN THE KNOWN UNIVERSE AND STAY BRIGHT UNTIL THE END OF TIME" written on it in four languages.

Gathering up #4, I go to the kitchen and attempt to wash some of it off and get the spuds started for dinner. Daughter #3 follows me in, dressed only in knickers and one sock, dragging her duvet behind her.

"Will it ever come off? Or will she have a blue tongue forever and ever?" she asks skipping around me as I struggle with the baby and the bag of potatoes.

"TOAST!" I scream back maniacally.

Have you ever noticed than in large families, someone is always making toast? In our family someone is always burning toast. I let Daughter #4 wriggle free and watch her hightail it out the door though I know that she should never be left out of my sight. Daughter #1 breezes past her baby sister and executes a very lovely pirouette; retrieving the toast and throwing it in the bin in one graceful move. Daughter #1 is very into ballet at the moment and tends to incorporate it into her every move.

"How do you start a teddy race?" asks Daughter #3 and, not waiting for an answer, goes straight into chanting "They're creepy and they're creepy. They're creepy and they're creepy. They're creepy and they're sneepy. The ADAMS FAMILY!" Daughter #3 has been blessed with vocal capabilities that give her the power of uninterrupted broadcast as long as she is awake. After five years, I still haven't found the OFF switch. I would be eternally grateful if only I could figure out the volume control.

"Oh wondrous mother," begins Daughter #1 performing a perfect arabesque while popping another piece of bread in the toaster. "Have you washed my socks for school?"

"Ready. Teddy. Go !" yells Daughter #3."The Adams Family! They're creepy and they're creepy. They're creepy and they're sneepy."

"Mamma! I really need my socks," says

A West Cork Life

Daughter #1 hanging upside down. She then tries out some stretching exercises whilst balancing a banana in one hand and three chocolate biscuits in the other. Along with dancing; food and boys are Daughter #1's main centres of interest- though not necessarily in that order.

Out of the corner of my eye I spy Daughter #3 start to climb onto the kitchen table, clearly headed in the direction of the sweets cupboard.

"You'd better get down or you'll fall off and die," says a lugubrious voice in the doorway. This is Daughter #2. She is ten, has a morbid fascination with death and destruction; and a unique sense of personal style. Her idea of appropriate Sunday attire is a pair of stripped leggings, a polka dotted shirt, and a woolen kilt. I am just about to gear up to a sermon about eating between meals when Daughter #4 makes her entrance. She is covered in sticky baby cream from her cherubic cheeks to her chubby toes. She is clearly delighted with the effect. She wears a grin from ear to ear and does a little dance to show her pleasure. She gets the three others rolling around on the floor howling with laughter. For an encore she gives me a big hug and decorates my clean shirt with long greasy white smears amidst hoots of approval from her sisters. It is at this precise moment that Himself steps over the duvets in the doorway and, clearly puzzled, asks when dinner will be ready. I understand the poor man's amazement when the only answer he gets out of me is: "TOAST!".

Happy B-Day To Me

I am absolutely flabbergasted. According to my calculations I am - gasp - 37 today. Check it out. Thirty seven years old, for Pete's sake!

How did that happen? I'm not meant to be thirty seven - not by a long shot. Not that I expect to be any ridiculous age like 15 or anything. No, I'm obviously all grown up, but I'd be more comfortable with something around 28 or there abouts. I could even settle for 30 and have fun getting all upset about it.

I tried complaining about it, but I got nowhere. Admittedly the first person I poured my Age Angst on was my father. It was a bad choice.

"Thirty seven? That's terrific!" he said cheerfully. "I'd settle for fifty any day." Thanks Dad. My mother was an even worse choice.

"I'm pushing forty!" I wailed over the phone.

What do you mean? Of course you're not," my mother answered curtly. I was about to point out that she, of all people should know my age when I realised that she was right. After all, how could I be pushing forty if she has never actually admitted passing that particular milestone. My mother stopped counting at 39 and is fine with that, thank you very much.

I then bored my friends with my disbelief at my age. The realists have pointed out that I have a husband, four daughters, a dog and two cats, and that it obviously takes quite a while to accumulate that much life baggage. Talk about hitting someone when they're down. That's exactly it! I howled as despondently as the Christmas shopper who has gone way over her credit limit without noticing. One minute I was fresh and young and worrying about my exams, and the next I was way past the "best before" date and worrying about Daughter #1's exams. Even my good friend Charlie (who is younger) tried to cheer me up by telling me how great I looked "for my age". Gimme me a break. I have a mirror. I also have a lifetime of old photographs of me grinning without any funny lines on my face. Some famous person said you end up with the face you deserve. Deep in my heart I knew that one day I'd end up looking like this - I just didn't think it would be so soon.

The killer shot came as we were shopping for my birthday party. I got the expensive trendy candles for the cake because I only had to buy two packets to make up the numbers. Had I got the cheaper brand I'd have had to go for three packets. The cake was a forest of multicoloured sticks that barely let the icing peek through. I was seriously considering using the hair dryer to blow the candles out, but the kids wouldn't let me. So I huffed and I puffed (and huffed and puffed and then huffed some more) and finally blew those suckers out. I swear - another ten years and we'll have to rent a flame-thrower to light the damn thing.

But one thing I'd like to know is: if I'm such a mature individual, why do I still feel like a six year old when 25 people serenade me with a rousing chorus of "Happy Birthday"?

The Never-Ending Bedtime

At the end of a busy day, all parents relish that blessed moment when the children are in bed and you can finally relax among adults. Peace descends like a goose down duvet and you can watch the telly, listen to music, or just stare blankly into space without being interrupted every ten seconds.

The problem is that as children get older that haven of tranquillity gets ever more difficult to attain. I can hear the screams of first time parents in the throes of colicky babies, screeching: "Now hang on there! Just one minute! What do you mean it gets worse?" Sorry guys. Yes it's true that babies can be

A West Cork Life

difficult to get to bed - but at least they don't talk back. Once children have command of the spoken word, putting them to bed becomes a family version of the Middle East peace talks. You have entered the realm of the Never-Ending Bedtime.

To start with, as children grow up their bedtime gets later. This means that while before you could pretty much be settled in by the time the Nine o'Clock News rolled around, now you are still shooing them out the door well after it's over. I suppose that the only way parents of sixteen-year olds get some peace and privacy is by going to bed before their kids do.

As kids get older they also get much better at stalling. In fact the relationship between how ragged they ran you during the day is directly proportional to how long they will hassle you in the evening.

Daughter #4, just coming up to two years old, has so much energy she puts the Durracell bunny to shame. She really should be studied by world powers as a potential energy source for when the planet's oil supplies run out. One hundred two-year-olds could probably power a small rural town. Yet once it's her bedtime she's pretty easy to handle as long as you get the ritual right. 1) Close curtain. 2) Arrange Big Bird, Moo Cow, Teddy and assorted friends and relations. 3) Secure bottle in mouth. 4) Tuck in covers. 5) Kiss good night. Do that in the right order, and you're pretty much in the clear. If she does wake up, the only problem you have is making sure you don't give Big Bird an extra bottle by mistake. Then again, she doesn't really talk yet.

Compare that with Daughter #3, who is six years old and fancies herself as an All-Talk radio station. She is very articulate for her age and does not stop gabbing while still awake. This can be somewhat taxing. When bedtime comes around she is relatively civil about it. But once in bed she could con the most hard hearted into reading her just one more story, getting her just one more glass of water, or singing her just one more lullaby. She also has a knack for remembering very important messages from her teacher about an hour after she's been put to bed.

At ten years old, Daughter #2 has honed her bedtime avoidance skills to a fine Art. When she was four she declared that she wanted to be an actor when she grew up. She takes her craft very seriously. Forget Drama school, the kid is getting all the training she'll ever need just avoiding going to bed. Her best performances (where she throws herself at your feet begging "Please, please, please." She'll never ask for anything again. She'll be perfect forever, if only she could watch Beverly Hills 90210 just this once.) are definitely worthy of an Oscar. Once she is actually in bed, her chosen speciality is the medical emergency. This child, who only hours before was the picture of health, can develop the symptoms of the bubonic plague within minutes of a good night kiss.

The Reigning Champ however is Daughter #1. Then again, she has had almost thirteen years of practice. I suspect the other three are busy taking notes. It is she who has truly mastered the two basic weapons for the Never-Ending Bedtime: negotiation and procrastination. Both are deployed before ever getting near a bed cover. Basically, first you negotiate as long as you can about exactly when you are going to bed. Every minute counts. Every friend and acquaintance's bedtimes must be reviewed for comparative fairness. The Geneva Convention may be invoked along with threats to call Childline. Once this line of defence has been exhausted (and you have reduced your parents to primeval beasts who can merely grunt "Bed. Now."), you then procrastinate as long as you can without actually moving in the direction of the bedroom. On a good night Daughter #1 can stretch going to bed over a three hour period.

Just because you got them into bed is no reason to drop your guard. This is the moment (generally about fifteen minutes into the film) when they begin to make their respective entrances for the Big Come Back. The subtlety with which an artful BCB is executed is worthy of Frank Sinatra in Las Vegas.

Memory plays an important role here. It seems to me that child and adult brains just don't work the same way. As the evening progresses, adults tend to forget more. But as children move into the night they remember more- mainly very, very, important things they absolutely have to tell their parents right now. Hunger also plays its part. The younger ones start starving and come in to beg pitifully for food- though they were in no way hungry at dinner. The older ones go in for commando raids. This entails sneaking into the kitchen, replenishing food supplies and making it back to base camp without being heard. If caught red handed feigned sleepwalking is an accepted tactic. This also works particularly well for slipping into your parents' bed and hogging the blankets.

Postpartum Awakening

Nipping into the pub for a quick coffee before picking up Daughter #1 from ballet class I bumped into a friend who had just been delivered of her first baby about two weeks ago. Her glazed eyes looked past me and she managed a wan smile as she mumbled something vague about the how the little fella wasn't really settling down yet. She reminded me of the last time I came home with my tiny new baby who filled me with such 24 hour joy (every four hours) that there was very little time left for anything else - including sleep.

Not sleeping is one of life's more interesting experiences. It does things to your brain and intrinsic character which point out just how shaky the solid persona we think we are, really is. Wake up every three hours, every night, for a few months; and the sophisticated, assertive, considerate, human being you imagine you are, turns into a blubbering idiot who gets hysterical if anyone leaves a towel on the floor. Your mind turns to mush if you don't sleep. Nothing seems to stick in there. It's as if the ERASE key had gone berserk. Short term memory is inexorably wiped out, and long term memory gets so jumbled as to become an embarrassment. The most basic information (Am I 35 or 36? What's my name anyway?) just zips out the back door of your brain. In fact, the back door is the only thing that remains open- well let's say slightly ajar- as you wander around on automatic pilot. Family and friends complain that you seem a bit vague. You ask the same question three times. For example: "Have you done your homework?" to your husband. If you have a brand new baby you are functioning on 5% of your total brain power. The other 95% is asleep.

I remember trying to stop Daughter #3 from yelling at Daughter #2 by telling her to sit properly and eat her dinner. Needless to say we were watching television at the time with nary a meal in sight. I once read that one of the most effective ways to breakdown a prisoner is sleep deprivation. This was noted as proof that torturers are just a bunch of sadistic perverts who like watching people in pain as they could easily extract a confession by simply keeping a person awake. Not true. In fact, torturers ARE a bunch of sadistic perverts who like watching people in pain, but they are efficient sadistic perverts. Sleep deprived prisoners couldn't read out a shopping list much less remember a secret code.

I tried to reassure my friend that one day she would sleep again. After all Daughters #1 and #3 had slept through the night by the time they were one month old. Then again Daughters #2 and #4 thought "night time was the right time to party", until they were well over a year old. My friend did not react. Instead she checked her watch and jumped off the barstool with alarming speed for someone fast asleep. Stifling a yawn she headed for the door mumbling vaguely that it was time to bathe the dinner and cook the baby.

ADVICE TO FIRST TIME MOTHERS

It's the middle of the night. The baby has been fed, changed, and burped and is still cranky. No matter what you do you can't get her to sleep. Here's a little secret: you're probably being too quiet. If you have a rocking chair (every new mother should be eligible for a rocking chair grant) don't rock gently back and forth. Really rock. Strong swaying with sharp jolts is what you're aiming for. If you don't own a rocking chair try singing Broadway tunes. Blues Brothers medleys are OK too. If you can get into the swing of it, try impersonating Ethel Merman.(HURRAH FOR HOLLYWOOD !!) If it doesn't work it's because you're not singing loud enough. Really belt it out. Once more with feeling! Dancing any Latin rhythm (cha cha, rumba, samba, lambada,) while carrying the baby is also a good trick. You may look silly, but believe me it really works. It also does wonders to help lift your spirits at 3 AM in the morning.

The Riddle of the Missing Sock

I have always hated laundry. Unfortunately as my family grew from one to four daughters, so did the pile of dirty clothes. Laundry and daughters correlates in a wriggly graph. First you get lots of laundry: baby grows, bibs and such. This decreases as the child grows to reach a steady sort of one pair of knickers per day/one set of pyjama a week, mode. Unfortunately, this proportion of laundry per daughter only lasts a few years. When the little darling reaches about five there is a sudden exponential growth in the amount of laundry one little girl can produce. It hits critical levels once the child reaches a stage in her development where she can both dress herself and play dressing up games. There are clothes everywhere. Daughter #3 can go through more outfits in one sitting of The Den than Diana Ross in concert. "Laundry" (i.e. discarded costumes) trails the mini-diva as she goes through her day. You can spend an entire evening just picking up after her. Then something really strange happens. When the child reaches the stage known to psychoanalysts as the latency phase, her laundry can dwindle to be almost nonexistent. Latency is meant to be characterised by a resolution of the Oedipal phase, but I reckon it has to do with never changing your socks. Daughter #2, who is ten, seems to truly relish living in dirty clothes. Given a choice, she would opt to sleep fully dressed in whatever she was wearing that week. Though I have no experience rearing a man-child I think that boys probably go through this phase as well. My experience with the adult man-child however, leads me to believe that they never grow out of it.

Laundry regains some of its vigour at adolescence, though if you look closely through Daughter #1's pile you will note that most of it is perfectly clean having not been actually worn but merely discarded on the floor as being unsuitable for whatever pressing social demands she has that day. I don't care. I figure that when you reach 12 you're old enough to do your own laundry. After all if you're old enough to argue the merits of being allowed to go to the local disco ad naseum, you're old enough to dye your own underwear pink.

However boring, doing the laundry has led me to do some investigative reporting worthy of the Beef Tribunal. It might not shake the financial and political world but it's going to do wonders for women around the world. No Ladies, you're not nuts. You did put a matched pair of socks in the washing machine and only one came back out. Loony as it may sound, one sock did just vanish. I know. I've worked on this. I have solved the riddle of the missing sock. I started by trying to find a matching pair. They were not easy to track down. In my house socks tend to split up and run away before they ever get near the laundry basket. However, I did manage to catch a pair huddling under the sofa and put them into the machine together. I then sat and watched. In they went together, singing "Going to the Chapel"; and out came one lonely sock wailing "It'll be lonely this Christmas." I've thought about this long and hard and I think I've worked it out. What happens is a conjunction of non-Euclidian geometry and centrifugal force. It's simpler than it sounds.

Tina Pisco

You know when the spin cycle goes into overdrive, emitting a shrill high pitched hum? This creates an ultrasound frequency (you can't hear it, but the hamster can) which punches a hole in the space-time continuum. The socks are sucked through it into a Sock 6th dimension where they presumably waltz around in unmatched pairs, until the machine spits them out again somewhere in our past or our future. That is why a sock is never lost forever. It will return eventually, though by that time you will have lost it's partner. This also explains why you find totally alien socks that don't belong to anyone coming out of the machine. They are not really alien- you just haven't bought them yet. Think of them as socks from the future.

TipToe Through the Tomatoes

Daughter #1 (13 going on 45) looks down at her plate in disgust and announces that she she's going to become a vegetarian. Lord, I'm tired. Do I really have to discuss the virtues of meat versus bean sprouts tonight?

"Why?" I ask, bracing myself.

"Well look at this!" she says poking an innocent lamb chop with her knife. "It's full of blood!"

Daughter #2 (ten going on Undead) smiles and says, "I love eating blood." She is our lugubrious daughter.

"Don't talk with your mouth full," I reply, noticing that Daughter #3 (five) has stopped eating and is giving her plate a frightened look.

"It's blooded?" she whispers, truly horrified.

"You can eat it with your fingers if you like," I say reassuringly, hoping to avoid a potential family disaster before turning back to Daughter #1.

"Mamma? I'm serious," she says in her most mature voice.

"Why?" I repeat.

"You already asked me that." Poke. Poke. Poke.

"Don't play with your food," I say. I see Daughter #3 stop in mid-bite to double check the acceptability of picking up her food .

"Not you sweetie," I say. Deep breath, and its back to Daughter #1.

"Listen being a vegetarian is an important decision. You'll have to think this thing through. It should be more than a whim," I proclaim, proud of the calm understanding-mother way I am handling this. I explain that you can't just stop eating meat. You need to supplement your diet with alternative forms of protein. I add that people become vegetarians for many reasons. Some people believe that in the face of world hunger it's stupid to feed a cow grass and eat the cow, when we could just eat the grass ourselves. Or something like that.

Some vegetarians still eat fish and chicken. Some won't touch a slice of cheese. Had she thought about leather jackets? Strappy sandals?

"I will not accept the 'I don't eat lamb 'cos sheep are cute and cuddly, but I'll eat lobster because they're ugly' school of vegetarianism," I conclude, pointedly referring to Daughter #1's passion for tearing lobsters limb from limb.

I'm obviously not getting through. Daughter #1 is still poking the now cold lamb chop.

As I take the poor thing and cook it some more (the chop not the daughter), I notice that the cauliflower, potatoes and tomato salad sit untouched on Daughter #1's plate.

That must have sparked some primeval reflex in the brain that turns a reasonable adult into a ranting impersonation of a despot. Only mothers have this. It is located somewhere in the region of the non sequitur reflex that makes us answer: "Have you done your homework and fed the pets? ", when asked: "Do you think Simon loves me?"

I hate to admit it but I totally blew my understanding mother cover by proclaiming that I'm not going to shop in specialty shops and cook separate meals because she thinks being a vegetarian sounds cool. Mea Culpa. I am rewarded with a heaving adolescent sigh worthy of Sarah Bernhard's more dramatic performances, and a few extra pokes at the now rock hard lamb chop. And this from a child who still has to be reminded to eat her vegetables.

ADVICE TO FIRST TIME MOTHERS

O.K. you've built an office complex from wooden blocks. You've pretended to eat a nine-course meal made out of plasticine. You've drawn dinosaurs, wicked witches, and what your kid thinks is a snail (though you had started out trying for a chicken). You're tired/hung-over/dead (because the baby kept you up all night). You can't bear to watch the Barney video again. You have no more games in you but your four year old still wants to play. Do not despair. I'm about to share a very important secret: Try playing Beauty Salon.

This is how you play it:

1) It is very important that you leave the room, knock on the door and come in again.

2) Say: "Excuse me, I have an appointment for a cut, wash, set, blow dry, permanent, dye job, and manicure. Shall I sit here?" Choose the sofa.

3) Lean back and close your eyes. Don't totally zonk out. The kid will notice and loose interest. As the child pretends to be the hair dresser make comments about the water

temperature, the colour of the shampoo, and the length of the cut. This will keep the action going. It's all you have to do in this game. If he/she says " All finished" after only 30 seconds remind her/him about the manicure. After a few tries you'll learn to keep up the chatter while practically asleep.

If you're too tired for even this minimum energy game try Road Accident. It goes without saying that you play the role of the victim.

However beware. This game requires that you actually lie down on the floor. Unaccustomed to the horizontal in the middle of the afternoon, you might become truly comatose and wake up to find the four-year old has redecorated the bathroom with bright red permanent magic marker.

Wedding Bells and Holiday Hell

I need a break. I think I'll join the navy - preferably in an elite corps on call 24 hours a day. It sounds restful. We made the mistake of going on a family holiday this summer and it nearly killed me.

Granted this particular holiday was a Grand Slam. This Triple Whammy of a vacation combined our first trip back to the city from whence we ran away two years ago (and where we had lived for twenty-plus years), with a sister getting married in a Cecil B. De Mille production that would put Ben Hur to shame. Friends and family flew in from three different time zones including the past. Two ferry crossings, interspersed with the joys of four kids crammed into a car hurtling down the M4, were the prologue and epilogue to our Holiday in Hell.

Preparations began sometime last Easter. After all, my washing machine can only take one 5 kilo load at a time. Having washed and dried enough clothes to equip a middle sized West Cork town, I found myself at the ironing board watching the Normandy landing commemorations from behind a mountain of clean clothes. As the commentator droned on about "logistics", my heart went out to those hardy D-Day planners. I knew what they went through having several "logistical problems" of my own. Here's one I'll share with you:

If a little girl/ woman wears clean knickers every day, and you have five such little girls/ women going away for seventeen days; how many pairs of clean knickers do you have to pack if you want to avoid doing laundry? Try it again with one trip to the laundrette included. If you enjoyed that problem, you can try the same thing with socks- taking into account that a variety of socks are needed for both informal and formal occasions, as well as the pink ones with the frilly border which match the flower print dresses. Once you've finished, try and calculate how many suitcases you need. Factor in the size of the boot.

You'd think that once we actually got there we'd kick back and relax. Not a chance. When we arrived at our destination the phone started ringing. It kept on ringing the entire time we were there. People are probably still ringing up who haven't realised that we've left. Every single one of them wanted to know about our new life in detail. I wouldn't be surprised if by the twentieth person we started sounding a little unenthusiastic about our Irish experience. I should have been clever and compiled a FAQ sheet and faxed it over before we arrived: "We are very happy in West Cork. The four girls are settled in school. We have bought a big house and are renovating it slowly. It is beautiful in West Cork. Yes- it does rain a lot. The people are friendly. The people are not all bigots. There are no bombs. We are perfectly safe - you're thinking of Northern Ireland. We really don't lock the car door. The car radio has not been stolen yet. We make our own: bread, jam, wine, etc. We are very happy in West Cork. It is in the southern part of Ireland." The holiday did teach me something of importance: If you want to see old friends properly, the only way to do it is for them to come over here for a holiday- Preferably one at a time.

Another important thing I learnt is this: I

have too many children to live in a city. No wonder most of my friends back there only have one or two. Four is madness when cars are zooming by, trams clanging along, and strange men lie in wait, lurking around street corners.

It doesn't help that my daughters have been enjoying the freedom of rural Ireland for two years. In fact Daughter #4, nearing three years old, learnt how to walk (Run actually. She has never walked.) by crossing fields rather than traffic. This makes her most unmanageable while waiting for the little man to turn green - the novelty of traffic lights having worn off in a few days. I have to admit that Daughter #4 was a gas to watch. "What's that noise?" (an ambulance, a motorbike, a plane, a fire engine) became her motto. She was puzzled by streetlights ("What are all those moons?"), and declared that the water, the milk and the butter were all "yucky". I'm thinking of leasing her out to Kerrygold and Bord Failte for P.R. purposes. Daughter #3, nearing seven, tends to wander off into shops and speak to complete strangers, forgetting that (unlike in our village) Mommy and Daddy do not personally know every inhabitant of the capital of Europe. I also had to explain to Daughter #3 that answering " How do you like being back in the city?" with "It's smelly"; though undoubtedly true, was not very polite. As expected Daughter #2 (eleven) and Daughter #1 (fourteen) loved it. This created it's own breed of problems as we drove across town in traffic jams to get them safely to whatever pressing social engagement they had cooked up each day. They were also reluctant to leave. The quiet beauty of West Cork pales in comparison to the rap pace of your shoes hitting the hot pavement of the streets. Not to mention the availability of international fast food outlets.

As to the wedding, it could take up an entire column just on its own. Suffice it to say that it added the joys and excitement of seamstress appointments across town in a traffic jam, picking up friends and relatives from the airport/station across town and in a traffic jam, and family feuds stuck in the middle of a traffic jam; to our already overflowing cornucopia of holiday fun.

Having packed, unpacked, repacked, unpacked, repacked (we changed accommodation while on holiday) and unpacked again; I've had about enough rest and relaxation as any woman can take. A week after returning from our summer trip to the Continent, all I can do is gasp in retrospect and thank my lucky stars that I somehow survived. Which is why, once the last load of holiday laundry was in,

A West Cork Life

I announced to my old friend the washing machine that the next time we decide to go on a family holiday - I'm staying home.

The Worst Thing About Having Kids

One of the great things about living in rural Ireland is that people do not go into shock when I mention that I have four daughters. In our village four is the average number of children. When I lived in the city (where people have 1.6 children per family) I was sick and tired of people's reactions. These ranged from disgust to concern about my mental health. The kindest would commiserate on my sorry state, adding with feeling that I must be very brave. Now I don't consider myself particularly cowardly but bravery had very little place in my decision to have so many kids. Not to mention the fact that they make it sound like the sort of bravery that the infantry needed during the battle of the Somme as they huddled in the trenches waiting for the Commanding Officer to sound the order to go over the top to certain death. I want to set this straight once and for all: I did not have children to compete for a long-suffering mother medal. I was not going for gold. I am certainly not a masochist. In fact I have made avoiding pain, even minor hassles, a life long crusade. No guys, I had children because basically I'm a hedonist. Call me crazy, but I enjoy them. Yes you get the night feeds, the nappies, and the crayon on the walls- but let's face it, Life is a messy business. I can't say that I enjoyed not having a full night's sleep for seven months but that's not the worst thing about having children. Forget the crying babies, the unsuitable boyfriends and everything that comes in between: For me the worst thing about kids is that they throw up in their beds.

The squeamish among you may want to stop reading this now. Likewise those who are soon off to lunch, or have just enjoyed a gastronomic meal. The stout hearted may continue. Kids throw up in bed. Though sound asleep, they do it with abandon. I have seen it described in pediatric textbooks as "projectile vomiting". I think you get the idea. It's all over the place:

The sheets, the pillow, the 45 assorted cuddly animals, the floor, the walls and, of course, the kid herself. She is covered from head to toe. If you think this tableau of horror is bad enough, may I add that it always occurs at precisely 3:30 am.

I'm a great believer in not doing today what can be put off until tomorrow (if you do this long enough you'll be surprised at how many tasks just disappear). However, being a mother has taught me that there are two situations that will not suffer procrastination: going into labour and the aftermath of a kid throwing up in bed. Every cell in your body is screaming at you to please not deal with this one just right now - but deal you must.

I'm still not used to it; though God knows with four kids the novelty should have worn off by now. Then again my kids are good at introducing new and improved versions of throwing up in bed, preferably while we're on holiday. Daughter #2 threw up in bed almost every night while we were in Crete. It did not bother her in the least. She remained blissfully asleep. I can't say the same for myself as we were sharing a bed that particular holiday. Daughter #1 however won the title of Queen of the Vomitorium after her performance on a short break in Ireland. She managed to throw up in the upper berth of a bunk bed. It was a very small room full of assorted holiday junk, open suitcases and sleeping bags. She remained asleep as did her little friend in the lower bunk and her sister who was sleeping in a cot nearby. I will not describe the scene.

Of course parents reading this column know that throwing up in bed is really only the second worst thing about having kids.

The worst thing is the thought that anything bad might ever happen to them. But that is too awful to contemplate, much less to mention.

THOUGHT FOR THE DAY

I hate to be categorical about anything but here goes: There is nothing in the world that is cuter than a baby. There I said it. I know someone who thinks Labrador puppies have cornered the cuteness market but she lives in New York City, so you'll have to excuse her. Nope, for turning grown men into great globs of quivering goo nothing beats a baby. Bring one to your next cocktail party and you'll see what I mean. Perfectly reasonable Yuppies stop discussing the equity market in mid sentence and gurgle. If the young human graces them with a smile, the room explodes into spontaneous applause. Granted there is always one skinny woman in a power suit who would rather discuss the equity market and who tries to get people's attention by saying things like "I've never understood why everyone makes such a fuss about babies. They drool." I have a sneaky feeling that she's the one who buys all those ridiculous baby vegetables that have become so popular in posh supermarkets. I bet she thinks they're cute.

END NOTES

Bits about goodbyes that didn't fit in anywhere else.

Goodbye to Father Eddie

As we drive up the road we can tell a major event is taking place. Cars going up to the village hall are blocked by a big four-wheel drive trying to execute a U turn while cars on their way down impede its progress. The logjam is at the gate of a field that has been opened up as a car park for the evening.

"Oh Man! It's total gridlock!" shouts Daughter #3 in a fake Jamaican accent.

"He's in the ditch! He's in the ditch" sings Daughter #4 as the four-wheel drive completes his turn and squeezes through by scraping the stone wall.

"We're in the ditch! We're in the ditch!" we

all chorus as I follow it up the road and past the on-coming cars. You get incredibly good at maneuvering large vehicles through tight spaces when you live in the back of beyond. Most roads only accommodate one and a half cars. You also get very good at skating on the edge of a ditch praying that your wheel won't slide, and that the ditch won't collapse.

A man in a reflective jacket waves a torch for us to turn into the field. West Cork men love to direct traffic and will do so at the slightest provocation. Being given the job of officially directing traffic gives rise to a wide range of gestures, winks, and hollers. There are always at least three men directing traffic, and fair play to them. Lining up cars in an unmarked, muddy field is quite an achievement. Getting the cars out again often requires bringing in a tractor to tow them. This, of course, necessitates more men, gesturing, waving, and hollering.

The hall is packed. All three hundred and fifty inhabitants of our village seem to be in attendance. Built in 1865, it was the one room schoolhouse for over one hundred years. On the back wall a large paper banner proclaims "Good Wishes Father Collins!" Father Edward Collins, or Father Eddie as he is affectionately known, has been the priest in our village for ten years. His involvement in village life is too long to list here but it ranges from the GAA to being a great dancer. It's thanks to Father Eddie that I can dance the Military Two Step. Last year the bishop tried to move him to another parish and within 48 hours a petition was signed by each and every person in the village (and a few visiting relatives, my parents included) to keep him on. So we kept Father Eddie for an extra year. But a few weeks ago he was called to serve in town, a new parish priest was appointed who would not be living in the village, and the priest's house was rented out to a family. It all happened in a flash and Father Eddie was gone before word filtered out to the likes of me, a pagan who does not attend mass.

Suddenly Father Eddie appears in the doorway. A round of applause greets his arrival. He pauses, feigns surprise, gives his head a shake, and grins. The clapping intensifies and people step out of the way pressing back until a small corridor is open. It leads to Father Sean McCarthy, official parish priest, now retired. Father Eddie is John Wayne as he strides into the room. One can easily imagine a spotlight following him down a red carpet as he works the crowds going into the Oscars. His face beams. He stops to shake a man's hand. He catches Father Mc Carthy's eye and winks. Father Eddie and Father Mc Carthy are worthy of Hope and Crosby now. Father Eddie points his finger with a "I'm going to get you look". The older priest laughs and points back. Father Eddie grins again and extends his hand. Then, at the last minute, Father Eddie drops a curtsy and winks. The crowd goes wild.

The speeches are wonderful. The audience is enthralled to hear about this man they love. They roar at the jokes: "You wouldn't think it to see him there -but this man has more Doctor of Divinities than you could imagine."

They smile when his gift with children is mentioned. The children cheer. They grow solemn and nod as his funerals are remembered. The big fire has a whole bale of peat briquettes roaring in the grate. In the damp heat of so many bodies I feel humbled by Father Mc Carthy's comment that Father Eddie had the gift of getting to know a person very quickly and never forgetting a face: "He will remember the names and conditions the next time he meets them. I'd say Father Collins remembers every person he's ever met and that's a gift."

Goodbye to a good man, so. They will miss you Padre, and so will I.

Blown Away by West Cork

With June just around the corner most of us are taking a deep breath, and readying ourselves to hit the season running. Things speed up incredibly over the summer in West Cork. The weeks are filled with a dizzying schedule of end-of-year school events, building projects, heavy gardening, First Holy Communions, and assorted weddings. Thank God for the long days- otherwise you'd never have enough time to fit it all in. Then again, maybe that's why we get so busy at this time of the year. After all if you want to do a bit of DIY after work in December you'll be up a ladder in the dark, in a gale. All this mad activity is compounded by the arrival of our visitors from abroad. Traffic jams clog the street. Shopping takes twice as long because of all the foreigners standing around the aisles reading labels, and weekend nights in town are so busy that most locals stay well away from it all until the Autumn, preferring to frequent rural pubs off the beaten track. Don't get me wrong- I'm not knocking the tourists. Having been one myself (complete with Aran jumper, tweed cap, wax jacket and wellies) I know how wonderful it is to choose West Cork as a holiday destination. Like many blow-ins I first came here on a holiday. It was a very wet week in November so I can't claim I wasn't forewarned. Yet after that first taste of West Cork there was nowhere else I wanted to visit. In fact, I desperately wanted to return. It was a longing I found incomprehensible yet irresistible. Less than two years later we'd moved lock, stock, and four daughters to a bungalow on Inchydoney Island. I still can't really explain it. I blame it on the faeries. Talk to many blow-ins and they'll tell you a similar story. They came on a short break to West Cork, and before they knew it they'd quit their job, sold their house and moved into a ramshackle stone cottage in the middle of nowhere. I know several families who came over for the weekend and kept extending their stay until it made more sense to move permanently. They say one guy was hitching to Kerry and stopped for a pint- he's been here fifteen years. There is a magical attraction that hits some of us almost the minute we get here. West Cork is full of "blown-ins", both Irish and foreign, and we all agree there's something magical here. We sit around talking about how lucky we are. We're called "blow-ins" but we really should be called 'blown-aways", because that's exactly what made us decide to make West Cork our home. We were quite simply blown away by the beauty, the craic, and the people. West Cork will knock your socks off. I'm really proud to live here and to be a member of the community. I've lived here for over ten years, and I don't regret it. I left the city and the fast lane because I was looking for something else in my life-something more. And I found it.

There have been blow-ins in West Cork for centuries, but the recent wave really started some thirty years ago. Last week one of the first of the "modern" blow-ins passed away. He was remembered by his friends and neighbours in Ardfield's lovely little chapel last Sunday. It was a beautiful West Cork day filled with sunshine and showers, with rainbows shooting out from the clouds above, and the sea glittering in the distance. He too was "blown-away" by West

Cork on a visit and decided to stay. He was as different and eccentric as blow-ins come; yet he fitted right in to the tiny rural community he loved so well. In a sense he showed us what it means to be a blow-in. He wrote the manual. He made it easier for the rest of us who came after him, looking for a place to build a new life; hoping that one day we could call West Cork home. The outpouring of grief and sense of shock felt throughout the area is a measure of his success. The rest of us can all only hope that when we leave this "land we love the best"*, we will be remembered with as much affection and sense of loss. Goodbye Luvy-we'll miss ye.

May 2003

* Thanks, again, John Spillane.

A Taste of Duende

The white witch of Cobh told me that I would die when I was 88. That didn't bother me one bit. In fact, I was rather chuffed. I was only 39ish at the time, maybe over forty - I can't remember. Anyway I wasn't even half way there and she said I would keep my mind till the end so I wasn't really bothered. I guess I would have liked to live to be over 90. Maybe even one hundred - but 88 and all my mind sounded pretty good and frankly with the moderate amount of abuse I have given this body I thought it wasn't that bad a deal really. It 's a good honest age to go. I could have died at 42 from lung cancer like Jacques Brel. Two

Tina Pisco
fat ladies is a fine age to die

The year I turned 44 I had a half-life party. A Big One. My entire collection of blue and white chinese porcelain got smashed that night. Not that it was a wild party or anything. Just a great one. Loads of people, loads of drink, masses of food, a session in the porch, a drumming session in the hall, dancing in the kitchen.

Poor Dave was quietly talking to someone when he leaned on the press and the whole thing came falling down. I was in the hall listening to the drumming when I heard it crash. In my mind I saw the press falling. I ran in and saw a thick carpet of broken blue and white porcelain, smashed glasses, and a few cups. My heart really did jump into my throat for a second. All that stuff- the beautiful 1950's glasses Manu had given me years ago, all the wine glasses, all the champagne flutes, all that beautiful chinese blue and white-All of it was totally destroyed. People gasped and braced themselves for an outburst.

Then I looked around and saw that no one was hurt. Wayne had cut his nose trying to catch the press- but it wasn't serious. I felt an immense wave of relief.

"It's only stuff" I said. And instantly I felt that wave of relief lift me as I I gave it all up - the tears I could have cried, the memories I could have rehashed. Maybe it was a message. Maybe I needed to know that I could stand there ankle deep in the debris of stuff that I thought meant so much to me and feel grateful. Like a big OUF.

So we had a great party and I turned 44. Halfway there. I decided that from now on I would count birthdays backwards. A countdown if you like. Not that I'll be 42 next month. I'll be 46 years old. But that's not interesting- that's just stats. Much more interesting is the fact that I have 42 years left.

Think about it.

"No!" I hear you plead. "Don't do that! It's too morbid! Who the hell is the white witch of Cobh, anyway? What does she know? You might live until you're 120!"

Well, first of all the white witch of Cobh is as good an authority as any in the "How long have I got to live" department. It's not like your doctor or your priest or your mother has got it more accurately. I might live until I'm 120- then again I could go for a walk and get hit by a flying cow. In fact, being hit by a cow is actually more likely where I live than being mugged, or hit by a bus; as the nearest bus stop is three miles away, but cows have been known to jump a wall and land on a car.

That's not the point. The point is to put a finite number on this whole life and death thing. It puts things into perspective. Instead of running around wondering "Am I going to die? When am I going to die?"- Put a date on death! Whip out that filofax. Don't just pencil it in. Write it in ink. It's easy to figure it out. The average woman lives to be around 75, average man is 72. Take an educated guess. Or go ask the white whitch of Cobh. She's great. You'll have a laugh.

Then when you've decided on a likely figure live with it. Live in the knowledge of a ball park figure of how long you have left. It's quite liberating really.

I've got 42 years left.

It's not bad. It's not too short but not so long that it seems infinite. That's 42 summers. 42 summers ain't bad, but you wouldn't want to waste too many (As Tom Waites says in Coppola's film, "Rumble Fish"). For example, I really like fishing-so a summer when I don't fish is definitely a wasted opportunity. I like sailing but I can skip a summer or two. On the other hand, lazing around in the sun is an opportunity that definitely shouldn't be wasted. If you're me you've got 42 summers left to do it in.

My Dad sent me an e mail once about a guy who roughly estimated how many Saturdays he thought he had left to live. He then took a big jar down to his basement and filled it with as many marbles. Every Saturday he went down to the basement and took out a marble. When the jar was empty he started putting one marble back in every Saturday. They were a bonus. Like frequent flyer miles.

In Spain they have a word: Duende. It's a hard one to translate because it is a state of being. Some people just have it. People with duende seem more alive, more creative, more prone to passionate joy. To sing with duende- like for example, a great Sean Nos singer- to dance, or play the guitar with duende is to move not only hearts but the very air in the room. Duende is that spark that ignites great artists, and great lovers. Duende is a positive power, a creative force- and yet it comes from a knowledge of death. A person with duende is one who is aware of death and burns that bit more brightly from knowing. Duende is like a blood-type. Someone who has it in his or her veins is likely to be creative, fey, prescient, spontaneous, captivating, melancholic, and volatile. It is by knowing death that they are so very alive.

I'm not sure that I want to count how many Saturdays I have left. Frankly, it seems rather anal and the likelihood of me keeping up any type of regular schedule is approximately nil- but you get the picture:

You figure out roughly how many years you've got left. You have a big party when you reach the half way mark (For those of you who may be well past that date: throw yourself a party anyway. Its retroactive). Then start to count down rather than up. The fact that you can pretend to get younger each year (Ask me how old I am? Mumble 42mumble) is just the icing on the cake.

And if you get it wrong: The extra years are a bonus.

This is an excerpt from a one-woman show I might actually finish one day. It was performed at the RandomAnimals Night in November 2002.

To order additional copies of "A West Cork Life" visit www.awestcorklife.com. Or email orders@awestcorklife.com